WEEKS

TIME WITH GOD

For Jacalyn
'It's words, words, words …'

TIME WITH GOD

Renewing your devotional life

Stephen Eyre

Inter-Varsity Press

INTER-VARSITY PRESS
38 De Montfort Street, Leicester LE1 7GP, England

© Stephen Eyre, 1995

All rights reserved. No part of this publication may be
reproduced, stored in a retrieval system, or transmitted, in any
form or by any means, electronic, mechanical, photocopying,
recording or otherwise, without the prior permission of Inter-
Varsity Press or the Copyright Licensing Agency.

Unless otherwise stated, Scripture quotations in this publication
are from the Holy Bible, New International Version. Copyright ©
1973, 1978, 1984 by International Bible Society. Used by
permission of Hodder & Stoughton Ltd. All rights reserved. 'NIV'
is a registered trademark of International Bible Society. UK
trademark number 1448790.

First published 1995

British Library Cataloguing in Publication Data
A catalogue record for this book is available from the British
Library.

ISBN 0-85110-886-5

Set in Palatino

Typeset in Great Britain by Avocet Typeset, Brill, Aylesbury,
Bucks

Printed in Great Britain by Cox & Wyman Ltd, Reading

Inter-Varsity Press is the book-publishing division of the
Universities and Colleges Christian Fellowship (formerly the
Inter-Varsity Fellowship), a student movement linking Christian
Unions in universities and colleges throughout the United
Kingdom and the Republic of Ireland, and a member movement
of the International Fellowship of Evangelical Students. For
information about local and national activities write to UCCF, 38
De Montfort Street, Leicester LE1 7GP.

CONTENTS

CHAPTER 1
THE BENEFITS OF A QUIET TIME

'Where is God?'

My faith seemed a burden and the future uncertain. God was silent. Or if he was speaking and guiding, I couldn't hear him.

We had come over to England from America for a short-term mission assignment. Our term was almost over, the lease on our house was about to expire and my contract was coming to an end. Things did not look good for a new ministry position on the other side of the Atlantic. The weight of providing for my family grew heavy. I knew I was supposed to trust God, but occasionally I struggled with a sense of panic.

At one point, as I called out to God with an urgent plea for help, a quiet urging rose within me that seemed to say, 'Do what you know.'

Whether that 'urge' was from God or whether it was my own personal insight, it was right on target. I had practised quiet times for years, but in the crises of the last few months had let them lapse. They were occasional and haphazard. So, in response to that inner prompting, I renewed my commitment and set aside time in my schedule. No immediate deliverance came, although eventually God opened doors for me, at just the right time. What did happen, however, was an ability to believe that the God who had brought me across the Atlantic could get me back. God was there after all.

I needed to have those quiet times because I need God. He is the one who makes sense of life for me, not just in times of crisis but in the day-to-day task of living. J. I. Packer writes,

> The world becomes a strange, mad, painful place and life in it a disappointing and unpleasant business, for those who do not know God. Disregard the study of God and you sentence yourself to stumble through life blindfold, as it were, with no sense of direction and no understanding of what surrounds you. This way you can waste your life and lose your soul.[1]

Quiet time is a tool *par excellence*, that aids us in the sort of knowledge of God that makes sense of life. A quiet time is like a looking glass; a sort of magic mirror, that lets us look into the deeper dimensions of life. In a quiet time we are able to see through the mirror to the spiritual depths of reality in which God is present. In a quiet time we can look not only at God but also at ourselves. Without the use of that mirror, God seems distant and the world around tends to lose its Christian character.

God is always meeting us, always caring for us and always directing us, but it is possible to be blind to his presence. Perhaps you have never tasted his presence in the first place. Or, it is possible that you have enjoyed his presence and then somehow slipped away. Either way, quiet times are important. As Israel was about to enter the promised land

Moses warned them not to forget the things they had seen or let them slip from their hearts as long as they lived (Deuteronomy 4:9).

I need the mirror of a quiet time to be a normal Christian. There is nothing spectacular about it when used in this way. It's like the mirror in the bathroom that I use when I shave. I suppose I could shave without it, but then the shaving cream gets smeared in the wrong places, I tend to cut myself with the razor and leave a few uncut whiskers here and there. Then there is the mirror on the dresser. I need to look in it to make sure that my shirt is tucked in right and my tie (when I wear one) is straight.

I need the mirror of a quiet time, not only to look at myself, but to look at life. The mirror shows me that God is really there, in the midst of life. As a Christian I believe that he is. But my experience of spiritual reality tends to come and go. Like most people I have been conditioned to believe that my personal value is dependent upon the level of my productivity. I am inclined to live a driven life aimed at accomplishing a list of goals that only grows and never shrinks. Who has time to think about God when there is so much to do? It's when I look in the mirror that I find it easier to have a living faith. As I look at my life in the mirror of my quiet time I believe in a different way, with a faith that knows and feels his presence. It is while having a quiet time that I muse to myself, 'Perhaps he is there after all!' When I look into the mirror, the push from inside seems to settle down. I continue to be busy, but not so driven.

I also need the mirror to look into the depths of my soul. On the lintel above the door of the ancient

Greek oracle in Delphi are the words: 'Know Thy Self.' This has proved to be good advice and a supreme challenge. A quiet time helps me to know myself. When I practise the discipline of a quiet time I am able to look beneath the surface of me. Who am I? What forces have shaped me? What needs, desires and fears direct me? Is God really at work within me? These are more than adolescent questions. We all need to address them from time to time throughout life.

When I look in the mirror of my quiet time, however, I am not trapped in some self-absorbed introspection. I see glimpses of me and glimpses of God. This is affirming and freeing. I find myself musing occasionally with a puzzled smile, 'Maybe I do have the gift of encouragement. Maybe God really is teaching me how to love.'

There is another side to looking at myself in the mirror. It is no less important and, at times, has been threatening and uncomfortable. These are the times when all the thoughts, motivations and unwanted emotions that I have stuffed inside of me rise up. Cupboard doors that have been boarded shut, swing open. Once, the things that I saw inside scared me so much that I stopped having quiet times for a while. In the end, I picked up the mirror again because continuing to look in it was the only way through to the other side of my fears. In the cultivated presence of God those pains in the depths not only surfaced, but were cleansed and transformed. Most of all, I grew in the knowledge of God. Like Job I was able to say what I couldn't have said before, 'My ears had heard of you, but now my eyes have seen you' (Job 42:5).

Discovering quiet times

While I am now an advocate of quiet times, it has not always been so. I was a Christian for several years before I had even heard of them. In the early years of my Christian life, I read the Bible like I would read a novel or a textbook. I was curious and I wanted to know what believing in Jesus Christ was all about. I didn't read the Bible religiously or to a schedule, I just read it. As for prayer, I prayed for things as I needed them, when I needed them. More often than not I was delightfully surprised when my prayers were answered.

I believe it was at a weekend conference while I was doing post-graduate studies that I was exposed to the idea of a daily quiet time. I didn't respond positively. I felt it was for religious people who were into rituals and traditions. However, over the next few years there was a change. Just as I began to understand that snatched meals on the run between classes weren't good enough to keep me healthy and provide me with the energy I needed, so I discovered that my sense of self and my relationship with God needed some order.

Along with a good dose of maturity, observing other Christians made me aware of my mistake. There were some Christians who seemed to have special substance to their lives. Being near them made me hunger to know God better. I didn't have to look long to discover something they all had in common; a commitment to have a personal devotional life. They were people who spent time with God. Knowing that it was wise, but with some reluctance, I made a commitment to have a quiet time.

Nothing remarkable happened when I started. At least nothing that I could see. The Bible didn't make any more sense than before, nor did I hear God's voice with any startling new clarity. I simply felt good about having a quiet time in the way I feel good after running for a couple of miles. I knew it was a good discipline that would contribute to my health if I kept it up. Eventually things did begin to happen and it became the looking glass of spiritual perception.

Now, after a couple of decades, having a quiet time is still a discipline. I do have to keep at it. But I have had time to see the benefits of spiritual knowledge, strength and endurance that it provides. And no matter what effort it takes to get it started and keep it going, it's worth it.

Getting started

The best way to learn what a quiet time is all about is to share it with someone else. I have been meeting with students in fellowship groups, business people in offices and church members in pews for a number of years to do just that. I make suggestions about how to spend time in quiet, point to a passage of Scripture, give guidance on how to reflect on God's word and then encourage prayer. Then we have a quiet time. There is a period of 'no talking' as we focus on being with God.

After we have gone through the spiritual exercises we talk about what has happened. I am always amazed at what emerges. Again and again I am delighted to discover that God is at work in me and my friends in ways that I never could have imagined. I have coined the phrase 'guided quiet times' to describe these meetings.

I wish that I could meet with you so that we could have a couple of guided times together. Since the chances of that are slim, a guided quiet time has been included at the end of each chapter. If you are to make the most of this book I suggest that you use these guided quiet times. All you need is a Bible and a pen and a desire to meet God.

For each quiet time there is an introduction that welcomes you into your time with God and sets a passage of Scripture in context. Then step by step you are led through Bible study, reflection, questions and prayer. It is possible to go through the quiet times in five or six minutes while you briskly fill in the blanks, but I doubt that you will get much out of them. Take twenty minutes or more and move through them in a leisurely fashion. Ponder the questions and write out your responses prayerfully. My prayer is that you will be delightfully surprised at what happens.

DESIRING GOD

My soul thirsts for God, for the living God.
When can I go and meet with God?

(Psalm 42:2)

Spiritual good is of a satisfying nature ...
And the more a man experiences this ...
satisfying sweetness, the more earnestly
will he hunger and thirst for more.[2]

There is something deep within us that longs for
God. It is the inner work of God's Spirit that all
God's children have. We have a divinely given
desire to seek him out and enjoy his presence. The
famous Westminster Confession, written in the
seventeenth century, puts it this way: 'The chief
end of man [and woman] is to glorify God and to
enjoy him for ever.'

But that inner hunger can grow weak unless it is
nourished and cultivated. Preoccupation with
day-to-day living can choke it out. If you are a
student, it may be a concern about results or
finding the right partner. If you are earning a
living or bringing up a family, it may be balancing
the budget or moving up the career ladder. Jesus
rebuked the church at Ephesus for having lost
their burning desire: 'Yet I hold this against you:
You have forsaken your first love' (Revelation 2:4).

As we begin this spiritual study, let us be clear that the first requirement for spiritual health is a strong inner desire for God. A. W. Tozer writes:

> Come near to the holy men and women of the past and you will soon feel the heat of their desire after God. They mourned for Him, they prayed and wrestled and sought for Him day and night, in season and out, and when they had found Him, the finding was all the sweeter for the long seeking.[3]

Unless there is an inner desire for God, all the praying, good works and Bible study are merely empty shells.

Today, as you begin, ask God to fan the sparks of love for him into a healthy, crackling fire.

Study

Look up these verses to see how important it is to desire God. As you look them up, ask God to speak them to your heart. Then write out in your own words what each one says.

Psalm 27:4, 81

Psalm 62:1

Psalm 63 (especially verses l, 5, 8)

Psalm 84 (especially verses 1-2)

Psalm 77:1

Proverbs 8:17, 34-35

Isaiah 55:6

Jeremiah 29:11-l4

Matthew 13:44-46

Reflect

1. Try to recall times when you enjoyed a strong
    hunger for the Lord. These may have been
    times in fellowship with other believers, or on
    a quiet walk in the country. List a few of them.

2. From what you have read and from your own experience list the reasons why it is important to hunger after God.

3. Spend time now seeking God to give you a heart that longs for him.

CHAPTER 2

WHY WE NEED QUIET TIMES

Several years ago I went to the Art Institute of Chicago. It took the entire day to walk through the section of European Art. I began in the fourteenth century and moved from room to room until I reached the twentieth century. The early rooms contain nothing but religious art, the last rooms, nothing but secular art. Somewhere along the way subjects other than God became more interesting to the artists.

Halfway through my day-long exploration of art, I was still in the centuries which were predominantly religious. My feet were tired from standing and my eyes from staring, and the images of one masterpiece after another were beginning to blur together. I left the Art Institute, went down the steps, crossed the road dodging a couple of cars on the way, and bought lunch nearby.

As I walked out, it seemed that I was not only leaving the building but moving from one world to another. Inside, everything I looked at during the morning had called me to ponder God. Outside, it appeared there was nothing intentionally calling me to reflect on God. Of course, nothing prevented me from thinking about God either.

Back in the world of the Institute after lunch, I resumed my pilgrimage. The seventeenth and eighteenth centuries were my favourites. Techniques had improved vastly and not all the art was religious. I actually found that a relief. Certainly there is more to say about God than painting religious pictures of Jesus being born or dying. Pictures of family life, still life, portraits and a good number of religious subjects were all exhibited together. God was in life, a part of life. Then at last into the twentieth century and modern art. Incoherent body forms in unrecognizable scenes – that's what a great deal of the art pieces seemed like. The works were harsh and metallic. It made me uncomfortable.

In contrast to the affinity I felt with the early European painters, something that reached across the centuries, I felt no affinity with the works of my age. There was no place for God. It was not that he was expressly denied or attacked, he just wasn't there. If I wanted to consider life in relationship to God in the twentieth century, then I would have to do it on my own. The artists' works didn't help me. In those rooms I felt out of place, uncomfortable, even lonely. My faith didn't fit.

That there has been an exclusion of God from most areas of our culture is not a new idea. But what did strike me in a new way was the effect that being in such an environment was having on me. In those rooms where the walls were covered with the works of Christian art and religious symbols it was easy to think about God. It felt 'normal'. In the rooms were there were no religious symbols or Christian references I felt 'abnormal'. My mind was taken in other directions and if I were going to think about God I would have to do it against the whole emotional tone of the paintings that surrounded me. In the twentieth-century rooms I felt immersed in spiritual blindness and the absence of God.

Of course, our culture is much broader and wider than a few rooms of modern art in some gallery. But the effect is the same. We live in a huge realm in which God has been intellectually, socially and institutionally excluded. This is true for the college campus, the market-place, and our free time. By the patterns of our lives and the unspoken expectations of those around us we are quietly, constantly and almost imperceptibly socialized into unbelief and spiritual darkness. It is as if, as Christians, you and I are standing on an escalator that is constantly moving downwards. Have your ever tried to walk up an escalator that is moving downwards? Educated by our social environment into a one-dimensional reality, it is hard for us to believe that anything beyond our five senses actually exists. Heaven, hell, God, the soul, prayer, these things aren't tangible, so we doubt that they are real, even if we are determined to believe they are.

In every aspect of society we are slowly institutionalizing the absence of God. As Christians we lament this. But while we lament it we are being damaged by it. Like everyone else, we go through each day with little occasion to call upon God. Unless we take conscious precautions, we too slip into a pattern of spiritual darkness. Despite our best intentions or even the depth of our convictions, we are affected. Like oxygen on metal, slowly, imperceptibly, the effect of our culture is to rust our souls.

Through the influence of our culture we develop

God-blindness. A colour-blind person can't see the colours red and green because the rods and cones in the eye are damaged. Many colour-blind people don't discover their problem until their teens. They have the words 'red' and 'green' in their vocabulary, but they are unaware that they have no personal experience of the colours. God-blindness works in a similar fashion. The rods and cones of our spiritual eyes are being damaged. We have the word 'God' in our vocabulary, but the experience of God is missing. And like colour-blind people, we go about our lives in the real world without sensing that something is wrong. When we practise a quiet time, we counter the forces of God-blindness.

As a teenager, my older brother was determined to become a pilot in the Air Force. However, when he took his physical, he discovered that he was not qualified. His eyesight was not good enough. He spent a day or two in deep depression, and then decided to see what he could do about it. Eventually, an eye doctor gave him a set of slightly out of focus picture-cards to look at. My brother was to stare at the cards until he could bring the pictures into focus. After a month or two of these eye exercises, he took the test again and passed.

In a similar fashion, a regular quiet time strengthens our spiritual sight enabling us to keep the reality of the unseen world in focus so we can meet with God and know with confidence that he is with us.

Avoiding God

Not only are there external spiritual pressures against which we must struggle, there are internal ones as well. There is something inside us that is predisposed against God.

Adam and Eve hid in the bushes from God after their sin. According to Genesis 3 God would often turn up in the afternoon for a walk in the garden. That time with God ceased as our progenitors hid from him and were then exiled from Eden. Our race moved further and further away. After Adam and Eve there was the disobedience of Cain, then the decadence that led to the flood; next there was the tower of Babel. From there it spread through all the languages and cultures of the world. It is our spiritual disease, we are all in the bushes because God makes us uncomfortable. The human race suppresses the knowledge of God and his constant call.

The history of Israel is a record of running away from God, even as there are the repeated calls to return. The worship of the golden calf and the broken tablets comes after a time of God's special care and powerful manifestations in the Exodus. As they were getting ready to enter the promised land Moses warned them, 'Only be careful, and watch yourselves closely so that you do not forget the things your eyes have seen or let them slip from your heart as long as you live' (Deuteronomy 4:9). It was a prophetic warning because that is exactly what happened. In the period of the judges the people of Israel repeatedly cried out to God for deliverance from their enemies and then promptly ignored him after he rescued them. Then for over two hundred years the kings steadfastly ignored the warnings of the prophets as God blessed them even in the midst of idolatry. Eventually God judged them by sending them into captivity in order to get their attention. From beginning to end God kept calling and they kept running.

This allergic reaction to God was even experienced by David, when he asked: 'Where can I flee from your Spirit?' (Psalm 139:7). Looking into his heart, he could see that despite his desire for God there was something in him that wanted to get away from God as well. He was aware that there is both delight and judgment in God's presence. 'Look away from me, that I may rejoice again before I depart and am no more' (Psalm 39:13).

I don't have to look very deep to find this dynamic of avoidance active in my own heart. In my early teenage years I didn't want anything to do with God. I left the church and God when I was fourteen and began to look for meaning in other directions. It was the Sixties, the Age of Aquarius, the era of universal peace and love. It was the era of the Beatles, the Rolling Stones and Crosby, Stills, Nash and Young. I grew my hair and played guitar. It was in the midst of this cultural ferment that my father married a woman who was outspoken about her faith in God. During the first year of their marriage, I avoided her as much as I could. I left the house early and came home late.

One evening two young men from my step-mother's church showed up at my front door and asked if they could come in for a chat. I allowed them to come in, but told them they were wasting their time. Sitting down on the couch they asked a few casual questions and then began to talk about God. Cutting them off at the beginning of the discussion, I informed them that l had given up my faith in God. I was sure that Christianity was irrelevant and scientifically disproved. They listened and didn't say much. I told them that I knew my life was empty and that I was in need of something. But God, the God of Christianity, was going to be the last direction I investigated.

Not long after their visit my resistance to God began to crumble. My car needed repair work and so my stepmother gave me a lift to work each morning. For a week I endured the raspy voice and haranguing message of a radio preacher that she listened to on the way into town. Most days I lay on the back seat, exhausted and hung over from the hard night of 'fun' I had had. Yet through the haze, that raspy voice had a ring of truth. It was as if somehow that old preacher knew me. Through his words, in some strange way, I was personally addressed. I found myself wanting to believe. It is a good thing for me that God is not put off by resistance. He continues to seek us even as we run.

I still find myself avoiding God these days, in a variety of ways. One of my favourites is the 'wait a minute' syndrome. I intend to sit down and pray. But, just before I do, a magazine article catches my eye. Or I remember someone I need to call. Before I know it the time set aside to pray is gone and there's something pressing I have to do.

I can even turn my own spiritual pursuits into a substitute for God. I remember spending a good part of one morning in serious study of the Scriptures. Suddenly I had a strong sense that God was sitting in a chair beside the desk. I felt a pull on my heart to put down my pen, turn to face him and just sit in quiet heartfelt worship. My response to this sense of call was irritation. I had determined that this was to be a study time. I wanted to wave away this call, grumbling, 'Not now God, can't you see I'm studying the Bible?'

Attending church and all sorts of religious activities can have the appearance of seeking God when in fact they are means of avoidance. Rousing worship services full of inspiring music and moving prayers are not enough to overcome this. Nor is being doctrinally correct a guarantee that we are OK. In fact, all of these can be dangerous because they allow us to cherish the illusion that we are spiritually growing when in fact we are in spiritual darkness. Isaiah wrote about outward forms of religious practice, 'These people . . . honour me with their lips, but their hearts are far from me' (Isaiah 29:13).

We practise outward religion because inwardly there is something about us that wants to avoid God. As we practise outward religion, our hearts are in darkness but we don't know it. We won't grow, God's light doesn't get in. Reading Scripture is merely an academic exercise in which we accumulate information about God. Worship is a mere routine; stiff and ritualistic. Good works done in the name of God don't mediate God's love even if they do give us a sense of self-satisfaction.

One of the seven deadly sins that Christians in the Middle Ages feared was sloth. Thomas Aquinas defined sloth as *'sorrow about spiritual good'*. It is a joylessness about God the source of all joy. It is despairing passiveness that gives up on seeking God. It is a cold sin that has passed beyond disobedience and rebellion. Sloth is what happens to us when we avoid God and then pretend that we are still religious.

The compulsive busyness of our culture is also a means of avoiding God. We are busy people. Many of us spend between forty to sixty hours a week at work. We spend ten to twenty hours a week in front of the television. The rest of the week is spent in the details of living; paying bills, cleaning the house, tending the garden, taking children places, and so on. Even as we keep up such a crazy pace, we lament it. Why do we drive ourselves? It's just another expression of our running from a divine encounter. If we slow down or are quiet for very long then the presence of God might just begin to get through.

The quiet revolution

Slowing down and being quiet then is just what we must do. The means to do that is the practice of a quiet time. As we slow down and become quiet we begin to counter the social pressures and inner dynamics of spiritual apathy. God is there to meet us if we open up. We need to take whatever steps are necessary to prepare for that meeting.

If you have never had a quiet time before, you are in for great riches, if you keep at it. Perhaps you have tried quiet times off and on over the years, but they have been more off than on. Don't be hard on yourself. The enemies and obstacles you face are formidable. When you sit down to have a quiet time, there are spiritual, cultural and emotional dynamics going on that you are hardly aware of. Your experiences of boredom, dryness, inconsistency, and all the other experiences you have had, are echoes of a great battle high in the heavenlies and in the depths of your soul. Whether you are aware of these dynamics or not, they converge on you when you sit down to be quiet with an open Bible.

When Moses asked to take Israel out into the desert for three days to worship God, Pharaoh was not pleased. Both Moses and Pharaoh knew that it was the beginning of a revolution and the end of Egyptian domination. That initial effort at worship was only the beginning of the redemption of the nation and there were many battles to come. If you determine to spend time in the worship of God, there will be many battles ahead for you too.

Christians have not had an easy time of it in the modern world. Nor will it get any easier. Churches that are merely filled with people who are busy doing Christian activities won't be up to the challenge. Nor will those Christians who limit the practice of their Christian faith to worship services on a Sunday morning. Churches that will be powerhouses for God will be comprised of individuals who are personally cultivating time alone with God in the weekly pattern of their lives.

FACING OUR RESISTANCE TO GOD

> Where can I go from your Spirit?
> Where can I flee from your presence?
> (Psalm 139:7)

While there is something deep within us that longs for God, there is also something in us that leads us to avoid him sometimes as well. Yet, it is not easy to see how we resist God. After all, aren't Christians supposed to want to be with God?

During a session of spiritual guidance, a young woman came face-to-face with her avoidance:

> 'I'm not sure what I am upset about, but I know it has to do with the way I see God,' she said. 'I realized that I keep God at a distance. I want to know him, but I don't. It's like Jesus is standing at the door of my life and I have it open just a crack. If I open it all the way, I am sure that he is going to burst in and tell me I have to be a nun. I hope that if I can just keep his laws and don't look at him directly, then maybe I can still live my life the way I want to.'[1]

There are numerous reasons for avoiding God. Several common ones are:

28

- we feel guilty and are afraid to face him
- we are disappointed by him
- we are angry at him and feel he has let us down
- we are afraid that he will make demands on us that we think are unreasonable.

Because we are masters of self-deception, it is easy to avoid God and not even be aware we are doing it.

A common pattern of avoidance is the 'wait a minute' syndrome. This is when you sit down to read Scripture, then suddenly remember that you need to take something out of the freezer, or find it impossible to ignore the letters on your table, so you put down your Bible to read the post, telling yourself you'll get back to the Scriptures in just a couple of minutes. But somehow you never do.

Another pattern is the 'I'm too busy' syndrome, when you go for a couple of weeks without an extended time with the Lord. Initially, the excuse is that there is too much to do today, and you'll get to it tomorrow. But the 'tomorrow' turns out to be a couple of weeks. When that happens, I know that I am avoiding meeting with God.

If we are to grow spiritually we must be able to discern the ways in which we personally avoid God, and know what to do about it.

Study

1. First let's look at the principle of avoidance from Scripture. Read Genesis 3:6–10. What is going on?

2. Read Psalm 53:2–3. Summarize what you understand it to mean.

3. Jesus confronted religious leaders who appeared to be seeking God, but in fact were not. Mark 7:6 says:

   He replied, 'Isaiah was right when he prophesied about you hypocrites; as it is written:

   '"These people honour me with their lips,
        but their hearts are far from me."'

What is Jesus' point?

Reflect

1. Ask God to show you the inner feelings or perceptions that cause you to want to avoid him. Spend a few minutes jotting down what comes to mind.

2. You need the help of God to see the typical patterns of behaviour by which your hiding is expressed. Ask God to show you.

3. Now, ask him to free you and release your heart to continue to grow in seeking him.

CHAPTER 3

WHAT IS A QUIET TIME?

Although it was years before I understood that it was possible to have a personal relationship with God, I did taste his presence prior to my conversion. I was eighteen and in my first year of college in the late 1960s. At that point my relationship with my father was not good. He didn't like my friends, the length of my hair, or my music. Conflicts and arguments were frequent. At one point Dad delivered an ultimatum: 'Get your hair cut, or get out.' I thought about this for a couple of days, calculated how much an apartment would cost, how much I needed to buy a new car and guitar equipment, and then offered a compromise. If Dad would stop hassling me about my hair, I would go to his new church with my stepmother on Sunday mornings. An hour a week seemed a bargain for free room and board.

What I didn't count on was the effect of those Sunday mornings on me. During the sermons there was that sense of being addressed personally again. It was almost a continuation of the radio preacher with the raspy voice. This preacher, that I didn't like, and didn't want to like, somehow had inside information on me as well. His words pushed their way inside me and pulled at me. I used to sneer at altar calls by religious fanatics, but when these altar calls were given, I clung to the back of the pew to stop myself from walking forward.

For several weeks there was a strange quiet that filled my car when I left church. It was as if there were another person there with me, a presence. I even turned off the radio and rolled up the windows to reduce the wind noise so that I could 'hear' the quiet that seemed to surround and fill me. After a couple of weeks of this I was ready to respond. My stepbrother invited me to a weekend conference. I went. When a call for commitment was extended, I heard the voice of the Lord directed at me. I felt called by name. I knew by the preaching of the Scriptures and the experience of his presence that he was alive and active in his world.

What I experienced in the car at the beginning of my Christian walk, the quiet presence of God, is what a quiet time is all about. A quiet time is the cultivated presence of God in the midst of our lives. Like a garden that we tend and fertilize, in a quiet time we set aside a time and place to tend our souls in the presence of God.

Meeting with God

A quiet time is a meeting with God. This is important to fix in our minds. Otherwise, a quiet time can become merely a set of routines and techniques that focus on Bible study and prayer. As we cultivate a quiet time, we must take seriously the pervasive theme of Christianity, that the presence of God is the birthright of every believer. When Jesus was born, the angel named him Immanuel, God with us. In his last words recorded by Matthew, Jesus says, 'Surely I will be with you always, to the very end of the age' (Matthew 28:20).

That promise of Jesus' abiding presence for all believers is the fulfilment of a special blessing that God offered to leaders of his people in the Old Testament. Abraham, Joshua, Samuel, David and Jeremiah were among those who knew and expected the presence of God. Moses' expectation of the presence of God is especially inspiring. After his encounter at the burning bush, the presence of God became the norm for his life and he was not willing to live without it.

Just after Israel had worshipped the golden calf, Moses returned to God to get another copy of the broken tablets. In their conversation Moses lamented the burden of leadership and asked for guidance. The Lord replied, 'My presence will go with you, and I will give you rest.' To this Moses responded, 'If your presence does not go with us, do not send us up from here. How will anyone know that you are pleased with me and with your people unless you go with us? What else will distinguish me and your people from all the other people on the face of the earth?' (Exodus 33:14–16).

As leader of the nation, he set up a tent on the outskirts of the Israelite camp and called it the 'tent of meeting' so that people could 'inquire of the LORD'. It was in that tent that Moses himself had the regular experience of meeting with God 'face to face'. When we have a quiet time, we are setting up a tent of meeting. We don't have to be a Moses, a Joshua or a David. We too can create a place outside the busy routine of life to meet with God.

34

This morning, when it was still dark outside and the rest of the family were not yet up, I looked out at the new snow on the ground, put a log on the fire and lit a couple of candles on the mantle. For a while I enjoyed the quiet of the house, even resisting the temptation to put a CD on my new CD player. Then I picked up my Bible. I am spending time in Psalms 1–10 right now. As I read through Psalm 4 the words of verse 7 seemed to lift off the page,

> You have filled my heart with greater joy
> than when their grain and new wine abound.

I found myself drawn, assured, focused and comforted. David meant those words when he wrote them three thousand years ago. One of the mysterious delights of the Scriptures is how they live across the centuries. As I read those words this morning, I found that I meant them. I didn't see any one, but I was reminded that God is here and it is good to know him.

The pursuit of God

Meeting with God – I make it sound so normal; as if it is something that you can do every day – no big deal. But don't misunderstand me. It is a big deal. And it is not so easy. A quiet time requires the pursuit of God. The author of Hebrews writes that 'anyone who comes to [God] must believe that he exists and that he rewards those who earnestly seek him' (Hebrews 11:6). Through the prophet Jeremiah God says to Judah, 'You will seek me and find me when you seek me with all your heart' (Jeremiah 29:13). We must reach out for God even as we sit down to be with him.

A. W. Tozer observed that 'contemporary Christians have been caught in the spurious logic that those who have found him need no longer seek him'. Nothing could be further from the truth. The paradox of the Christian faith is that those who know him are those who seek him. Tozer writes,

> Come near to the holy men and women of the past and you will soon feel the heat of their desire after God. They mourned for Him, they prayed and wrestled and sought for Him day and night, in season and out, and when they found Him, the finding was all the sweeter for the long seeking.[1]

The Psalms are inner glimpses of those who knew and pursued God in the Old Testament. David writes:

> One thing I ask of the LORD,
>   this is what I seek:
> that I may dwell in the house of the LORD
>   all the days of my life;
> to gaze upon the beauty of the LORD
>   and to seek him in his temple.
> > (Psalm 27:4)

In another psalm he says:

> My soul thirsts for God, for the living God.
> When can I go and meet with God?
>
> > (Psalm 42:2)

In Psalm 84 we read:

> My soul yearns, even faints
> for the courts of the LORD;
> my heart and my flesh cry out for the living God.
>
> > (Psalm 84:2)

It is the power of the Psalms that they not only record such a pursuit of God but that they stir up that desire in us as well.

The language of Christian spirituality is filled with words like desire, hunger, pining, seeking, restlessness and yearning. Bernard of Clairvaux wrote, 'We taste of Thee, O Thou Living Bread, And long to feast upon Thee still; We drink of Thee, the Fountainhead and thirst our souls from Thee to fill.'

Jonathan Edwards, the leader of the first Great Awakening in the American Colonies in the eighteenth century, wrote of the satisfying nature of spiritual good. The more a person experiences this satisfying sweetness the more earnestly he or she seeks it.[2]

A quiet time can be a place of experiencing the satisfying sweetness that Edwards and Bernard of Clairvaux refer to. We create the time and space to allow the presence of God's Spirit to break through. It doesn't happen all the time, but occasionally something rises up – a yearning towards God breaks out. I never know exactly why it happens, but there is a sense of being drawn. Like slow-burning coals that become a crackling fire when they are fanned, an emotional desire breaks out and pulls my heart into a yearning for God. Perhaps that is what the apostle Paul was referring to when he wrote that God's Spirit in our hearts cries out, 'Abba, Father' (Galatians 4:6). During those times we are able to know cognitively and effectively that we belong to God. There is an in-filling of affection and gratitude that brims over in our hearts. When that happens we need to close our Bibles, put away prayer lists and just sit in worship.

We must never be satisfied with a faith that sees God as an object of knowledge or even with our present knowledge of God. Paul prays for the Ephesian church that 'God . . . may give you the Spirit of wisdom and revelation, so that you may know him better' (Ephesians 1:17). It is always possible to know God better than we do and to be more enriched because of it. We need to press on, and having a quiet time is an essential way to do that.

The practice of spiritual disciplines

Even as I encounter God and pursue him, I have found that the knowledge of him can elude me. The longer I was a Christian, the more I became frustrated with the disparity between my knowledge, actions and thought patterns. I discovered that doctrinal formulations alone were not sufficient to keep me in healthy fellowship with God. (Jesus' encounters with the Pharisees and Sadducees illustrate this point.) Nor were shaking experiences with the Holy Spirit (I have had a few of them) enough to sustain me in daily holiness.

Four years of Bible college filled me up with volumes of scriptural truth. I read lots of books about God in addition to reading the Bible. But just because I had read a profound truth in Scripture or in some great Christian book, it did not mean that I could appropriate it in the daily patterns of my life. I needed help to encounter God's truth in a way that would leave me transformed. As I struggled with this, I discovered spiritual disciplines. Not formerly open to such ideas, in the pursuit of God I found myself open to strange words like solitude, silence, fasting and meditation. And these not as a means of achieving salvation, but for spiritual growth in God's free gift of life in Jesus Christ.

One of the dangers of talking about spiritual disciplines is that they conjure up images of hooded monks chanting in the early hours of the morning. In the minds of most of us the disciplines are only for those who have left the world and chosen to live an ascetic lifestyle. They are really most impractical for us 'normal' folk. In reality, spiritual disciplines are tremendously practical. They can be used, in fact need to be used, by those who experience the daily challenge of living out their Christian lives in the work-place.

Spiritual disciplines began to make sense as I looked for avenues of growth. They filled my quiet time with meaningful actions. Throughout this book, we will be focusing on several of those disciplines which fit easily into a half-hour quiet time: silence, the discipline of getting quiet so you can listen for the Lord; solitude, the discipline of setting aside some place where you and the Lord can be alone together; Bible study, the discipline that helps you grasp the meaning of the biblical text; meditation, the discipline that helps you penetrate and embrace the Scriptures; and prayer, the discipline of asking God for help for yourself and others. While I won't specifically be addressing worship or confession, if you practise a quiet time for very long these disciplines will begin to show up naturally (supernaturally) as the Lord meets you.

As I began to practise spiritual disciplines in my quiet time, one benefit I discovered was that my spiritual senses developed. For a long time, I didn't even know that I had any! As I spent time in meditation, looking to God with the eyes of my heart, while I didn't see him with my physical eyes, I knew he was there. There was a sense, a real sense, in which I saw him. And as I stopped doing all the talking in prayer and began to listen with spiritual ears, I didn't hear a voice, yet I found that answers came to questions I was struggling with. And more than just answers, I discovered a restful, even tender quiet that filled me. I knew that God loved me and that he is good.

Spiritual desire

The human heart has an innate hunger for God. It is a hunger that is often disguised as something else. G. K. Chesterton said that every knock on a brothel door is really a knock on the door of heaven. Gerald

May, a psychoanalyst, writes, 'After twenty years of listening to the yearnings of people's hearts, I am convinced that all human beings have an inborn desire for God. Whether we are consciously religious or not, this desire is our deepest longing and our most precious treasure.'[3] Quiet times allow us to address that hunger properly.

Just as we can't live without daily food, we can't live without constantly, repeatedly feeding on the life of our Creator and Saviour. God's Spirit inside believers creates a taste for him. Through his work inside our hearts, we come to relish his word. It becomes 'sweeter than honey' (Psalm 19:10) and spiritual milk (1 Peter 2:2) that causes us to grow up in our salvation.

How do we get the sustenance of God's life into our lives – our daily bread? The pastoral image of the twenty-third psalm points the way. We allow ourselves to be led into green pastures. God wants to take us to a quiet place where there is leisure to eat and still waters from which we can drink. Psalm 1 also gives a clue. The person who is blessed by God, doesn't walk in the ways of the ungodly, but, like a tree planted by a stream, has the constant nurture from the extended leisure that meditation on God's word requires. Both the sheep in the pasture, and the tree by the stream are images of quiet rest in the presence of God – a quiet time.

When we have a quiet time, we feed our souls; we lift our eyes beyond the here and now to the eternal; we lift our hearts from the mud of mixed motives to the unsullied Good; we look past the dark god of this age to the God of eternal light. The Lord is present;

all creation sings his glory. In our work, our family, our recreation and whatever we do we can know his presence. Unless we practise the discipline of quiet time, however, we will probably miss the meeting.

THE LORD'S ATTENTION
Matthew 4:23–24

Yet I am always with you;
  you hold me by my right hand.
You guide me with your counsel,
  and afterwards you will take me
    into glory.

(Psalm 73:23–24)

Sunday morning worship is important to me. I love being surrounded by people who sing hymns in a heartfelt way and who pray as if they believe that their lives depend on it. On most Sundays I come away uplifted and refreshed.

But I have found that Sundays are not enough. I need personal time with God as well. Just me and God. I need to know that he knows my name and is involved in the details of my life. I need his personal guidance.

Peter, Andrew, James, John and the other disciples must have had the same need as well. After being with the crowds, Jesus often took them aside for personal attention and private instruction. In the Sermon on the Mount we have the most complete and concise summary of Jesus' direct teaching of his disciples.

The good news is that such personal instruction is not limited to the first disciples. It is available to his disciples in every generation. It is available to you and me. All that is required is that we respond, read and listen.

Approach

Someone once commented that God doesn't have favourites but he does have intimates. Write a couple of sentences to God telling him that you want to be close to him and know him better.

Study

1. Read Matthew 4:23 – 5:2. News about Jesus spread throughout Galilee as he began his ministry. What was Jesus doing and saying to collect such crowds?

2. The crowd Matthew mentions was a large one. What do you think would be some of the reasons people had for seeking Jesus?

3. Consider other significant events related to mountains in the Scriptures. Look up the following passages and write down a summary of each one.

Exodus 19:20 – 20:1

1 Kings 19:11–13a

Matthew 17:1–7

Acts 1:10–12

4. What is the possible significance of Jesus teaching on a mountain?

5. Why do you think Jesus might focus on his disciples rather than on the crowd?

Reflect

1. What would it be like to be following Jesus among the crowds? Write down what you might feel emotionally and physically; and what you might hear and say to others.

2. Consider your own motivations towards Jesus Christ. What would be your reason for being in the crowd?

3. Just as Jesus called the disciples out from the crowd in order to teach them, Jesus wants to give you the same personal attention. How prepared would you be to listen if Jesus called you out from the crowd to receive his personal instruction?

4. Write down the hindrances to being a disciple that you find in your heart. Now turn them over to the Lord.

Prayer

Ask God to give you the attitude of a disciple, with a listening ear and a responsive heart.

Pray that Jesus' kingdom would continue to expand and that many would hear his word and receive his healing touch.

CHAPTER 4

SETTLING IN GOD'S PRESENCE

If we are going to create a space and a place to meet with God then we are going to have to set aside time. That won't be easy. Most of us feel that we already have too much to do and not enough time. How in the world are we going to fit in the time to be with God?

As we have been discovering, if we are to practise a quiet time then we are going to have to challenge the mind-set that we have inherited from our culture. We are going to have to think differently about time, for in our materialistic age we think 'Time is money'. The cardinal principle of time-management is that unplanned time is the means of failure, while controlled time, governed by our purposes and priorities, is the key to success. Exactly.

Time is the key to success. But as Christians with a broader view of life, we must say the focus of our culture is too narrow, too limited and too secular. The real issue is not, 'Time is money' but *time is holy*. If we let the principles and priorities of material success govern us then we will become spiritually impoverished. When I don't control my time, then time for God simply vanishes in the flow of a day, a week or a month. We need to seize the time. *Carpe diem.* We need to order our time for our spiritual health.

God's time

God thought that time with him was so important that he built it into the Ten Commandments: 'Remember the Sabbath day by keeping it holy' (Exodus 20:8). This gift of time was to celebrate his creation of the world according to Exodus. And later it was also to celebrate his redemption of Israel from slavery in Egypt (Deuteronomy 5:15).

More than one day in seven was set aside for Israel. God established five feasts every year, two of which were a week long. The order of the feasts was: Passover and Unleavened Bread in March/April, Pentecost and the Feast of Weeks in May, Tabernacles in September/October, Trumpets in late September and the Day of Atonement in early October.

And not only were days and weeks set aside, but years were holy as well. God set aside one year in seven, the sabbatical year, as a holy time devoted to rest and worship. In addition, each forty-ninth year was a Sabbath year, followed by the fiftieth, the Jubilee year, a holy time when all debts were forgiven and all slaves set free.

What is the message of these feasts? Surely one message is that God is the centre of time. God creates time, meets us in time and orders time. Therefore, the use of our time is to revolve around him. By having these designated days, weeks and years, the centrality of God was experienced repeatedly by Israel. And by celebrating these feasts, they would learn something essential about God. More than a burden, these were reminders of God's saving care. They were truly holidays. People were set free from toil and debts, to rest, worship and celebrate.

Israel missed the significance of this gift of holy time. At first, the gift of holy time was ignored. Subsequently it brought the condemnation of the prophets. God, through the prophet Jeremiah, commanded the wayward nation, 'Do not bring a load out of your houses or do any work on the Sabbath, but keep the Sabbath day holy, as I commanded your forefathers' (Jeremiah 17:22).

Or, conversely, the gift of holy times was turned into a legalistic burden with ridiculous restrictions. By the time of Jesus people couldn't cook a meal or walk over a mile on the Sabbath. What was missed by Israel, which we too may miss, is that God was building into the very structure of the life of his people a protected time in which he could be worshipped and enjoyed.

Daniel understood the essential issue. Living in the midst of the pagan world of Babylon, he established a pattern of praying three times a day: morning, noon and evening. He ordered his day around time with God. He found it necessary to keep that pattern, even when it resulted in his being thrown into a den of lions.

The Christians of the Middle Ages ordered time around the worship of God. The *day* was ordered around the prayer times of Prime, Sext and Vespers. The *week* was organized around Sunday. The *seasons* were organized around the Christian festivals of Christmas, Easter, Ascension and Pentecost. And the *years* were organized around the birth of Christ, BC and AD. Without clocks and wrist-watches the churches were the primary means of time-keeping.

Not only were there bell-towers to call people to worship, but churches had the only mechanical clocks. You could look up to the church tower in the centre of town and find out what time of day it was.

As we move into the modern era, the sense of time ordered by God is gone. Holidays are merely vacation times, Sundays are days for sports and recreation. Christmas and Easter are times to buy and give gifts and unveil our latest fashions. None of these retain the sense of making time in our lives so that we can be with God. Somehow we need to counteract this secular drift, to reorder our priorities and to find ways of recapturing time for God.

Seizing the time

So how can we recapture time in order to be with God in the way that we need to nourish our souls? What is involved in building up time patterns which allow us to meet with God?

We must choose to set aside holy time

By choosing to set aside time in our schedules we can experience fellowship with God. And in doing so we can learn to see our time focused on God not as an interruption in our day, but as a reminder that all of our time is under his Lordship.

My father-in-law used to take time at lunch to read Scripture and pray. When others went out to eat, he pulled his lunch bag and Bible from his desk drawer. He usually had half an hour alone with the Lord. A working mother in our church finds that her only hope of quiet is to get up half an hour before every-one else, in her case that means 5:30 a.m. College students have flexible schedules and can often find an hour or so between classes.

I have found that making room for a regular time in a schedule is initially almost an act of violence. I must seize the time and set it aside. Something else will have to give way; an hour of sleep, social time with your friends, a programme that you want to watch. And once you have set aside this time, other important things will spring up to fill it. But if it all seems too much of a sacrifice, think about how you always find time in your schedule to eat several meals a day. More then ever people are setting aside time to exercise their bodies. Shouldn't we be able to find time to feed our souls as well?

We must seek to have regular holy times

In our meeting with God we need a pattern that we can count on. Our regular time of meeting with God needs to be anchored into the routine of our lives. The prophet Daniel used the meal times of morning, noon and evening. That may not be realistic for you. But you need something.

Most people find mornings the best, before work. There is a precedent for that in Scripture. Mark records that at the very beginning of Jesus' ministry, before sunrise, Jesus got up to pray (Mark 1:35). But perhaps lunchtime fits best with your schedule, or maybe you can control your time in the evenings so that you can spend time nourishing your heart on the Lord.

My regular times with the Lord have varied over

the years. Depending on where we have lived and what my career has involved, I have had different meeting times. My best times are in the mornings when I can get into work before anyone else arrives. After time with the Lord I have a sense of being prepared to face the rest of the day in the presence of God and with the strength and wisdom that he provides.

There are several stages involved in establishing a regular routine. The first is a novelty stage where there is a sense of excitement that you are doing something new and fresh. After a while that soon turns to boredom and resistance. At that point you may be tempted to give up, and your quiet times may seem stiff, routine and even legalistic. But if you keep going, there will come a sense of certainty and responsive anticipation of meeting with God.

Once your routine is established there is something nourishing in just knowing that at certain times in your day and week you are going to be able to seek the Lord. Your inner person becomes spiritually open and responsive as soon as you sit down to begin your time with him.

We need extended holy times

Not only do we need regular times, we also need extended holy times with God that allow for a sense of rest. In Israel, the Sabbath was set aside so that a whole day could be given over to rest and worship. And the feasts of Unleavened Bread and Pentecost were set aside so that a whole week could be given over to rest and worship. How much we can learn from such provisions of the Lord!

Devotional times for most people I disciple vary from fifteen minutes to forty-five minutes. That describes my normal pattern as well. I have found, however, that this is not enough to satisfy my spiritual hunger completely. When I take an hour or three or even a whole day to be with God there is a heavenly homesickness that breaks loose within me. It is in those extended times of being with the Lord that I sense the depth of his peace, the freshness of his Spirit, the tender affection and quiet of his presence. I find myself longing and reaching out to God. Often there is a quiet, satisfying softness and yet a reaching out as something inside me yearns for more.

These longer times are important because there is just so much going on in life that can't be dealt with in regular daily meetings with God. In the daily time there is just about room for the reading and study of Scripture, a few minutes of quiet seeking and then prayer for the issues of life that need to be brought before God.

What we can't deal with adequately in our routine times is the in-depth study of Scripture. Nor can we adequately face the hurts and pains of the past and present, or the mortifying (the lost art of grieving over moral failures without falling into self-condemnation or self-pity) of our sins. Without the help of extended times, it is difficult to slow down enough to hear what the Lord may be saying about the root issues of life. In extended times you may find you need the first hour just to identify and unload your anxieties so that you can become quiet enough to settle in the presence of the Lord.

How do you go about setting aside extended time?

One way is to use the Sabbath as it was intended. After church and the Sunday lunch, and maybe even a look at the paper, there is ample time to be with both the Lord and the family. While I was a theological student I became convinced that I shouldn't study on Sundays, even if there was a test on Monday. Not only did this give me times to worship and fellowship without the pressure to get back to the books, but I was reminded that, in the end, my grades and my learning where gifts given by God, not achieved by my own determined effort.

What do you do in an extended time? This can vary greatly. If you are used to meeting with God on a business basis, reading a passage of Scripture, and offering a few prayers for the day, then meeting with God in a sense of holy leisure will seem strange. Initially you may feel like you are wasting time. There is often a 'restlessness barrier' that you will have to break through. But on the other side of the barrier there is a rich, full rest.

We need a sense of continuity in our lives to cultivate holy time

I am not merely referring to the specific time when we sit down to be with God, but about our daily routines.

When our daily patterns are disrupted, keeping time set aside to be with God is difficult. I have noticed that students frequently comment on how they struggle spiritually during summer vacations and holidays. I find that myself too. Somehow in the change of routine the time and space created to meet with God vanish and it may take a while before I am able to re-establish a helpful routine. In our need for routine I see the value of the spiritual rule of the monastic orders. Meeting with God flourishes in a sense of rhythm and order.

We need to be flexible in our holy times with God

This may seem like a contradiction to the preceding principle of continuity. But the reality of modern life for most people is one of constant change. We cannot cling rigidly to some ordered devotional routine and then throw in the towel when the routine is broken.

Students' schedules change from term to term and are interrupted by holidays and vacations. Working lives are affected by business trips, holidays, job changes and deadlines. Family lives are in constant flux because of the burdens and pleasures of bearing and bringing up children.

We can cope with changes in the routine of our lives if we have determined that time with God is important. Perhaps our morning time with God may be disrupted during the holidays. And perhaps we may go for a couple of days without reading Scripture and praying. But if we are determined, if we are convinced in our hearts that meeting with God is important, then we can be alert for times in the day when we can take an hour or two to be alone with God. The issue here is not to be legalistic with ourselves and upset if we don't get our devotional time when we want.

The secret is to set our hearts to be gracious toward ourselves and determined toward God. We need to settle ourselves in the presence of God.

SETTLING IN GOD'S PRESENCE

My heart is not proud, O LORD,
    my eyes are not haughty;
I do not concern myself with great matters
    or things too wonderful for me.
But I have stilled and quieted my soul;
    like a weaned child with its mother,
    like a weaned child is my soul within me.
O Israel, put your hope in the LORD
    both now and for evermore.

(Psalm 131:1–3)

We live in a busy world, and we are busy people. But if we are going to spend time with God we will have to slow down.

We have to stop doing things all the time in order to create a space in our lives to be with God. You have already begun to do this by working your way through this guide.

But stopping outwardly is not enough.

Once you have stopped outwardly, you may discover that you are still busy inwardly. Your mind is full of things you need to do, or should have done: people to phone, letters to write, errands to run. The list is endless. If you are going to meet God, then you have to get past these inner demands to sit worshipfully in his presence.

How can we be still, inwardly and outwardly?

56

First, don't ignore the demands upon you. It is because they are important to you that they have such power. Richard Foster writes:

> We can give up the need to watch out for number one because we have One who is watching out for us. I sometimes like to picture a box in which I place every worry and every care. When it is full I gift wrap it, placing a lovely big bow on top and give it as a present to the Father. He receives it, and once he does I know I must not take it back, for to take back a gift once given is most discourteous.[1]

However we do it, we need to give over our concern to the Lord. Sometimes I picture myself writing out a list of pressing issues on a 'to do' list and then handing it to the Lord.

Study

Read the following verses from the Psalms:

> Be still before the LORD and wait patiently for him;
>   do not fret when men succeed in their ways,
> when they carry out their wicked schemes.
>
> (Psalm 37:7)

> Be still, and know that I am God;
>   I will be exalted among the nations,
> I will be exalted in the earth.
>
> (Psalm 46:10)

Why is it important to be still?

2. Read Exodus 14:13–18. How was Israel still and active at the same time?

Reflect

1. As you sit before the Lord, give over your responsibilities and your concerns and fears. Write down all the things that you have to do.

2. Now, either give the list to the Lord to place it in his 'in' basket, or put the list in a box and make a gift of it to the Lord.

3. How do you feel after so specifically turning over your cares to him?

4. What difference will this make in the way you face today?

CHAPTER 5

FINDING A QUIET PLACE

Several years ago I spoke at a conference at a church in Beverly Hills. Taking a walk between sessions, I noticed that there were three churches on nicely landscaped grounds in the space of two blocks on one side of Santa Monica Boulevard. On the other side of the boulevard and across the tracks was Rodeo Drive and the business district. When Beverly Hills was laid out in the early 1900s the developers didn't want to allot any land to churches because they didn't generate profits or tax revenue. However, Will Rogers, a film star during the early days of the film industry, objected that you couldn't have a community without providing for the community's spiritual needs. The developers reconsidered. At that point, the only space they could find to put several churches was on the strip of land across the tracks that had been set aside as a public park. So that is where they squeezed in the churches. Such is the modern mind. Creating space for God is a grudging afterthought!

However, church buildings used to be welcome in the heart of business sections. At the centre of many old cities there is usually a town square with a town hall. Opposite the town hall, in several directions, you will find a number of church buildings. In fact, in Medieval Europe, the word 'city' was originally a technical term to refer to towns that had a cathedral.

Cathedral building has ceased and skyscrapers now replace cathedrals at the heart of the modern city.

Meeting places in the Bible

A place to meet with God is a prevailing theme of the Bible. If you are to cultivate the practice of a quiet time, then you need to find a place to meet with God.

In the Old Testament, when God was encountered at a certain place, that place became marked as holy, *a place set apart for God*. Shortly after Abraham entered the promised land God appeared to him with the promise, 'To your offspring I will give this land' (Genesis 12:7). In response, Abraham built an altar. After Abraham divided the land with Lot, the Lord appeared to Abraham again with the promises of countless children and the land to live in. Again Abraham built an altar (Genesis 13:18). And, when Jacob had an encounter with the Lord in a night of wrestling that resulted in a dislocated hip and his name being changed to Israel, he made an altar. Jacob commented, 'How awesome is this place. This is none other than the house of God; this is the gate of heaven' (Genesis 28:17). In response he set up a stone to mark it.

The practice of marking holy places continues in the Old Testament with ebenezers, or stone markers, which commemorate God's help. Joshua set up pillars of stones when they crossed through the Jordan river. The stones were to be reminders that God had stopped the Jordan: 'These stones are to be a memorial to the people of Israel for ever' (Joshua 4:7).

Ultimately the sense of a holy place was expressed in the presence of the ark of the covenant and its location in the temple in Jerusalem. When Solomon dedicated the temple he acknowledged that the heavens can't contain God, yet prayed 'May your eyes be open towards this temple night and day . . . so that you will hear the prayer your servant prays towards this place' (1 Kings 8:29).

In his discussion with the Samaritan woman at the well (John 4:21–24), Jesus affirms Solomon's insight that God is not to be localized to a specific place. God is not to be limited to a mountain or to Jerusalem. More important than the place is the manner, 'in spirit and in truth'. Even so, places have their significance in the gospels. Jesus himself seemed to find the Sea of Galilee a favourite place to minister and the desert a favourite place to pray. He began his ministry by going out into the desert for forty days (Luke 4:1–2), and he frequently returned to desolate places (Luke 5:16).

At the end of history, the place to be with God will be the New Jerusalem in the new heaven and earth. There is a whole chapter in Revelation picturing what it will be like. The description contains a fair amount of detail which initially seems hard to understand. The point, I believe, is not in the symbolic meanings of the precious gems or streets of gold. We are given the details to help us see that place itself is important and precious. In our final state we are not to float about in some disembodied spiritual nether-world up in the clouds. The holy city is a real place. There will be our place and the dwelling of God. In that place our fears, hurts, needs and desires will be satisfied. In the centre of the city there will be no skyscraper or cathedral, but the throne of God.

Meeting places in Christian history

The priorities of the previous Christian era are reflected in the church buildings and cathedrals that were the heart of the town and country. Go to any major European city and there, in the centre of town, and no doubt one of the major tourist attractions, will be a massive cathedral.

Being an American, cathedrals were something I had only read about in history books until our move to England. On my initial visits to cathedrals, I was surprised at how deeply I was affected. First there was the feeling of being overwhelmed by the size of the building and the beauty of the artwork. Then there was the sense of history that was striking: eight hundred years or more of continuous worship. And then there was an awareness of holiness; God was honoured in these places. They had been the building efforts of an entire community for hundreds of years. Clearly God was the priority. These were places set aside to God, they were holy.

In earlier times, not only were cathedrals designated as places to worship God, monastic houses were set up to allow entire communities to pursue God. In the sixth century St Benedict founded the first enduring religious community. Over the centuries the Benedictines, Augustinians, Franciscans and other orders followed, providing a focused and ordered environment in which God could be sought.

We don't think much of religious orders today. But Christians of other ages created both cathedrals and orders, not merely out of religious extravagance. They knew the need for well-defined and protected places that encouraged ways of thinking and living for the benefit of their spiritual growth. We too need structures in our lives that provide a safe place to meet with God. The busyness of our lives in the pursuit of money, recreation and education tends to displace any space in our lives where we can meet him.

Finding meeting places

How can we find such holy places where we can meet with God? Cathedrals may be great settings, but they can't be the norm. There are two types of place that I look for. One allows for sitting; I study and reflect on passages from the Bible and then sit in quiet listening prayer. The other allows for walking; I do my serious intercession during walks. And while I am walking I also allow my mind free reign to think about God and the issues of life that I am facing.

It is popular to say we can worship God anywhere, that we don't need buildings. However true this may be, there is a sense of place that pursuing God requires. C. S. Lewis once observed that God always seemed less real to him in an hotel room. My own experience confirms Lewis's seemingly strange observation. It is the familiar place that creates a context for spiritual focus. When we move, or when we must find somewhere new for our quiet time, there is period of transition before we can settle into the familiarity of being with God.

The spiritual and the physical are interconnected in ways that we may not completely understand. When we meet with God regularly in one place, the physical surroundings take on a special significance. As we are surrounded by them, they become friends that invite us into the presence of God and remind us that he has met with us there before. They also give us a sense of anticipation that he will continue today and tomorrow in our holy encounters.

A holy path

When I was a new believer, I found that the beach by the Gulf of Mexico where I walked in the evenings was a holy place to me. Just walking along the shore with the wind, waves and sand put me into a seeking mood. I found it easy to reach up and out to the Lord in prayer. When I moved away from the coast, I went through a period of grief and experienced a sense of separation from God. Eventually, however, I found that walks in the woods and streets around my house worked just as well. The woods just took time to become the familiar setting of expected encounter. During our stay in England we lived about a mile from the underground station. My walks to and from the station became great times of prayer. We lived in Northwood, a suburb thirty minutes north of London on the Metropolitan Line. The streets were wide and there were pavements all the way. By about the time I crossed the High Street and turned on to Station Road I had gone through my list and could say a fulfilled 'Amen'. Those walks were spiritually some of the most powerful of my life. When I reviewed my list for one autumn, I saw that every request on the page had been granted! Not far from where we are living now, there is a park with a path around a lake. I find it a great place to walk and pray.

A holy seat

My places for study and reflection have varied over the years. But whether at my desk in the office, a small room in the back of a church, a little cubicle in a local retreat centre, or a quiet corner in a restaurant like McDonald's, a table upon which I can spread out my journal is the important physical requirement. To be able to study the Bible, to be able to consider the issues of my life before the Lord, to discern the hand of the Lord in the events of my life, these are the important spiritual activities.

There have been periods when the local McDonald's was my favourite place! I found I could be alone there for an hour or so with very few distractions and a great sense of solitude. Whoever thought a table at the back of a restaurant could provide all this? But I have had some of my best insights about God, life, writing and myself there.

Wherever we choose to sit down with the Lord, the key issue is to be where we can relax and spend time leisurely.

In a meeting place with God there are certain qualities that are important.

A special place

We need special places to be nourished by the Lord – something out of the ordinary. If I am using my desk for business, making phone calls and writing letters, I find it difficult to make the transition to the sense of quiet necessary to seek the Lord. That is why walks or a café have been so important to me; they are places that break the routine and help me, physically and mentally to know that I am coming away to seek the Lord.

Of course, sometimes the desk is the only place that is appropriate. If this is the case, I try to clear the top, stuffing unfinished work in drawers so I won't see it. The clear desk and the open journal and Bible then become the ebenezers that remind me that I am preparing to meet with God.

A protected place

We also need protected places. If we know that interruptions are impending then it is hard to cultivate the focused heart that seeking the Lord requires. If I know that the phone is going to ring, or that someone is going to knock at the door, or the post is going to arrive through the letter box, then I find I am waiting on people or things rather than on the Lord.

One way to overcome such distractions is to get to my desk before the 'official' start of the day, before the post arrives and the phone rings. Time and space can then come together in a way that helps me know that they are exclusively the Lord's, that this is now the time and place to be with God.

A familiar place

And finally we need familiar places. There needs to be a sense that God has met us here before. As my feet hit the path of my normal prayer walk, there is an awareness that my whole body, as well as my mind, knows that it is time to pray. When I sit down in the chair that I use for meditation and reflection I find myself being drawn into worship as my heart reaches out to the Lord.

Conclusion

Recently Jackie and I felt the need to have extended time with the Lord. Any place in our house was out of the question because of the activity level of our children. There was no way we could be undisturbed for several hours. But if we can arrange to go out for an evening of entertainment, which we do fairly often, then we could arrange to go out for a Saturday morning of prayer. So we did.

We arranged care for the boys, reserved a room at church and spent a Saturday morning in prayer. The church room was perfect. It was a special place, different from the ordinary routine; it was a protected place where there were no phones or responsibilities, and it was a familiar place because our church is where we have repeatedly experienced times of spiritual enrichment.

Discipline is the operative word. We need patterns of thought and behaviour which draw us away from an improper focus on ourselves and the world, to a proper focus on God and his word. We must give thought to when and where we actually sit down to spend time with the Lord. Because the patterns ordering our time and place with God are no longer provided by our culture, we must seek to establish our own.

BEGINNING OF THE GOSPEL

Mark 1:1–8

New things are exciting. *'Bigger'*, *'better'*, *'newer'*, are the phrases the advertisers use to get us to sit up and pay attention to their product. New cars shine, smell fresh and have all the latest extras. The problem with new things, however, is that they get old. Today's new clothes will be out of fashion next year. And besides that, they stop holding their shape and begin to look shabby. New cars lose their shine, get dented and cost increasing amounts to maintain, to the point where we eventually want to get rid of them.

But what if there was something that was always new, always fresh, and just beginning, something that never got old? What if the excitement of new ideas and fresh opportunities kept on for ever?

That is what the gospel of Jesus Christ is like. It began two thousand years ago with the ministry of John the Baptist and Jesus. But, because it is about the eternal God who is the source of new life, it never gets old.

When we read about the events of the gospel in the New Testament, we are never just reading about things that happened long ago and ended. What we are reading about is the start of the ministry of Jesus which, because he rose from the dead, will continue for ever. This means that you and I can get in on the action. We too can be a part of this world-changing, life-changing good news ministry of Jesus Christ.

Approach

When you enter a cinema, your sense of enjoyment is enhanced because you are in a dark room with no windows and therefore outside distractions are cut off. In addition, the screen is large and you are surrounded with sound. Your sense of encounter with the Lord will be heightened if you put yourself physically and emotionally in a place where you can focus on the Lord. Seek to focus on God and write down every distraction that comes your way for the next five or ten minutes.

After you have written down your distractions, ask him to prepare you and empower you spiritually to enter into the Gospel of Mark. Write out your prayer.

Study

1. Read Mark 1:1–8. In verse 1, Mark writes about the beginning of the gospel. Describe what is going on in the following verses, noting such things as the people, places and times mentioned.

2. In Israel the normal way of dealing with sin was through a sacrifice offered by the priests at the temple in Jerusalem. Why do you think that people were coming out to John?

3. We don't use the term sin much in our culture any more. What is sin and how does a sense of sinfulness affect people?

4. John is in the desert, calling people to get ready for the coming One. How would the desert setting help people in Israel get ready to return to God?

Reflect

1. Imagine yourself in this crowd gathering to hear John's message. What feelings do you have?

2. John called people to turn away from their sins in order to get ready for the coming of the Messiah. What things do you need to turn away from to grow in the knowledge of Jesus Christ?

3. Some people think the first verse is the title for the whole book of Mark, not just the opening verses. Read it again and in your own words write out what it says.

4. If the gospel began in Mark and is still continuing, that means you and I can participate in it! Consider and write down how you would like to experience the spiritual truth of these verses in your life now.

Prayer

Pray through your personal prayer list.

Pray for our world, that the message of Jesus Christ would bring a turning from sinfulness to the forgiveness that he offers.

Pray that the church would continually prepare itself to welcome Jesus.

CHAPTER 6

GETTING ALONE WITH GOD

If you are like me, getting up in the morning to have a quiet time is difficult. I found it easier to get up for a class in college or an early morning breakfast meeting than getting out of bed for a quiet time. We may tell ourselves that we struggle with a consistent morning quiet time because we don't want to get out of bed. However, I believe that the real issue is something else. We struggle with getting up for a quiet time because we avoid being alone. (That is why having a quiet time at any time of day can be difficult.) When I get up for a class or a breakfast meeting I am spending time with people. When I get up to have a quiet time, I am spending time alone.

For most of us, being alone and loneliness go hand in hand, and loneliness is painful. Psychiatrists and clinical psychologists speak about it as the most frequently expressed complaint. It hurts to be lonely.

There is something about the way we live that encourages loneliness. *The Lonely Crowd* by David Riseman was a landmark book published in the 1950s, describing the lonely experience of life in the modern city. We can be lonely even in the midst of a crowd.

Listening to the radio, I sometimes think that most of the songs could be summarized by the phrase 'Please don't leave me alone.' The current gener-ation, dubbed the 'X generation', is described as a generation alone; they have had to face the consequences of 'baby boomer' parents who struggle to keep their marriages together in a culture of marital turbulence and two-income consumerism. The experience of growing up for them has been a sense of growing up alone.

From the root of loneliness comes destructive fruit. On the one extreme, there is the loneliness of the addict who seeks to kill the pain with drugs. On the other, there is the loneliness of a TV watcher who stares at a screen and makes no real personal contacts. In an attempt to cope with the pain of loneliness we may work harder, play harder, perhaps drink or take drugs, and rush into relationships that offer the potential of intimacy, but in the end fail to deliver the goods.

Despite what we may think, loneliness and being alone are not synonymous. If we are to cultivate quiet times, then we need to learn the difference. Loneliness is being alone and experiencing an inner emptiness. The other side of loneliness is solitude. Solitude is being alone with an inner fullness. If we are to have a regular quiet time, we must learn to move from loneliness to solitude.

What is solitude?

Solitude is being alone on purpose

Loneliness happens to you. A lonely person is someone who feels isolated and cut off from others against his or her will. A child who can't find friends to play with, a rejected lover, a new person in town – these are lonely situations. When we feel lonely, we feel as though we are victims.

In contrast, solitude is something you choose. When I put on my running shoes and head out of the door, I am choosing to be alone. I am looking forward to the benefits that come from the exercise and the opportunity to let my mind roam free as I pass by a lake, glimpse the squirrels, and duck under tree branches. I am alone, but I am not lonely.

For some people, the choice for solitude is fairly easy. Their temperament inclines them to get away from people. Jung termed them 'introverts'. For others, being alone is almost unthinkable. They draw energy from being with people. Jung termed them 'extroverts'. Solitude is still important for extroverts, but it comes at a greater cost and must be managed in small doses.

Solitude is being alone for personal growth and accomplishment

As a high-school student, I hated to spend time in my room doing homework. My grades suffered. When I got to college, it was study or perish. I found time to get to the library. Alone, away from my friends and other distractions, I actually began to get passable grades and learn a few things.

Those who are successful learn how to be alone. Whether it is an artist with a canvas, an author staring at a page, a teacher making out a lesson plan, or a business person reviewing accounts, these things must be done alone. From that time alone, a painting can be put on public display, a book may be published that many will read, a teacher can stand in front of a class of students, and an accounting can be given to the stock-holders and the board of directors.

Solitude is being alone for personal renewal and refreshment

Being mildly extroverted, I like being with people. But after a day of counselling and meetings, I am exhausted. I need time in the evening alone before I am ready to face another day.

One of the problems with our modern world is that it is difficult to be alone. We have phones in our cars so that we can talk while we drive. And then there is the radio. When we come home there is the television. This continual exposure to voices talking or singing at us creates an emotional deficit. In the end we have nothing to give, and we seek to take from those, who like us, have little to give. We are not refreshed.

The soul has power to replenish if given relational space. Going for a walk alone in the woods, taking time by yourself on the back patio in the summer twilight, or lying beneath the stars, these things bring inner renewal. Of course, if we spend time alone while we restlessly wait for others to call or come over, there is no refreshment. We only feel deprived and our energies are further depleted. The benefit comes when we *choose* to be by ourselves in solitude.

Solitude is being alone in order to enhance our relationships

Someone has described marriage today as two ticks

without a dog. Facing each other with a sense of need, marriage partners bring to their marriage a sense of loneliness with the expectation that the other will take it away. This leads to great frustration because, in the end, no-one can take away our loneliness. We must face and transform it ourselves.

The frustration similar to that of lonely marriage partners is what many of us feel in all of our relationships. The closer the friendship, the greater the expectation, and consequently the greater the burden. In our loneliness, our relationships become greedy and needy, clinging and dependent.

When we are able to choose solitude, something happens to our relationships. Instead of expecting others to give, we have something to give. When we don't have to be with people out of a sense of need, then our hearts are open to receive, however much or little our friends and lovers can give. There is a sense of open freedom and relaxing peace in being together without demands.

Solitude is being alone in order to be with God

Solitude equips us to be in relationship with other people. We come away from them in order to come back to them. Solitude takes on a different character with God. In solitude we choose to be alone with him.

Imagine being in a room with a loved one, watching television while other people carry on conversations. If you want to enjoy being together and have a personal conversation of any depth, you have to get up and leave the room. When we choose solitude, we are choosing to leave the room to be with our loved one.

When we are alone, we can discern God's presence. We discover that he was speaking all along but we just couldn't hear it because of all the distractions. Martin Luther wrote, 'I do not know it and do not understand it, but sounding from above ringing in my ears I hear what is beyond the thought of Man.'[1] As I sit in solitude, I frequently find that inner fullness that wells up from inside and pulls me into a deep sense of communion with God.

In solitude with God, all the other benefits of being alone come together as well. We find a sense of purpose that stimulates our creativity while bringing personal renewal and enhanced relationships. When we add solitude to efforts to set aside a time and place to be with God, we have the necessary framework for a quiet time.

The biblical basis of solitude

In both the Old Testament and New Testament, those who grew in the knowledge of God were called to times of solitude.

Abraham's experience of solitude began when he was called from his home in the region of Babylon. God said, 'Leave your country, your people and your father's household and go to the land I will show you ' (Genesis 12:1). Although Abraham left with his wife and a few servants, he was going into a life of solitude, choosing to follow God and leaving the familiar life in which he grew up. The night when God gave Abraham the covenant promise of a child and countless offspring, or years later when he walked up the mountain to sacrifice his promised son – these too were experiences of solitude. Abraham chose to be with God in ways that set him apart from everyone else and led him into a life of faith.

Solitude was a constant part of the life of Moses. His first encounter with God at the burning bush was one of solitude. He alone saw the bush and heard the voice. When he received the Ten Commandments on Mount Sinai he spent forty days alone with God. The tent of presence in which he met daily with God was also a place set apart to be alone with God. At the end of his life, alone, he ascends a mountain in order to get a glimpse of the promised land and then to pass on to the other side of death.

How much of David's life must have been spent in solitude? As a shepherd boy he learned to trust God as his shepherd while watching the sheep on the fields of Judah. His skill with the sling that would eventually slay Goliath came from this time by himself with no-one but the sheep. Later, when he was king, his life continues to demonstrate the fruits of solitude as he writes psalms of intense feeling, deep thought and faith.

Jesus' ministry begins with a call to solitude as the Holy Spirit takes him into the desert for forty days. He emerges from that time alone with God after overcoming Satan, ready to proclaim the kingdom of God. Throughout his ministry he would go off alone to pray. Luke writes: 'Jesus often withdrew to lonely places and prayed' (Luke 5:16). In teaching the disciples about prayer, Jesus emphasizes solitude. 'But when you pray, go into your room, close the door and pray to your Father, who is unseen. Then your Father, who sees what is done in secret, will reward you' (Matthew 6:6).

Following Jesus, the disciples were led into the experience of solitude. It began for them in a way similar to that of Abraham. They were called from their family fishing business to a life of dependence. '"Come, follow me," Jesus said, "and I will make you fishers of men." At once they left their nets and followed him' (Mark 1:17–18).

It is not in the first disciples that we see most clearly the way of solitude, but in the apostle Paul. Shortly after his conversion, he writes that he was led into a period of solitude in Arabia in which he was instructed by the Lord (Galatians 1:15–17). On several occasions he was put in prison. Although his isolation was imposed upon him, he turned it from a time of loneliness into fruitful solitude. In Ephesians he refers to himself as 'a prisoner of the Lord'. In other words, he trusted that the Lord himself was working through his jailers. By his exercise of faith he escaped being a victim. He knew that God had a purpose for him. From those prison experiences, he wrote letters that have spiritually nourished millions of Christians for almost 2,000 years.

The last book of the Bible, the book of Revelation, was given in solitude. John was confined on the island of Patmos. While he was worshipping the Lord, he heard a voice, saw a vision, and was given a glimpse of the end of history.

Choosing to be alone

Just as we must seize the time in order to have a quiet time, so we must seize ourselves and our relationships if we are to grow in solitude.

We must get away from people

At the least, we must get away from those people who want to talk to us. We may be able to go into a room and close the door at home. Or we may have to get out of the house. As Jesus taught us, we need to find our own 'closet'.

It helps to let family members know that we want some time alone. Initially this may be greeted with puzzled looks, but most families will adjust. Room-mates will as well. One high-school student I know puts a small cross on his door when he doesn't want to be disturbed. His parents know to leave him alone, and that he will come out when his quiet time is over. Perhaps, if you are a college student, your room-mates can get the message you want to be alone when you sit on your bed or at your desk with your Bible and journal open.

With some determination and creativity we can find a way. I can be alone nicely in a shopping mall or in the coffee shop of a book shop near by. No-one talks to me and I can pray or ponder.

We must get away from entertainment

Our time and space to be alone with God is aggressively consumed by our entertainment devices. We spend time watching or listening when we could be by ourselves. If we merely got up and turned off our televisions and videos, our excuse of too little time to be with God would vanish immediately.

Televisions also create difficulties for solitude because, for most of us, they are in the family or living-room which is the focal point for family gatherings. It seems almost disloyal to get up and walk out of the room in order to be alone.

Televisions also create problems for a sense of solitude, because their sound goes through walls, around corners and up through ceilings. We have our television in the basement. This may not be possible for you. Even with it in the basement the sound at times comes up through the floor. To cope with this I have a set of headphones. Putting them on with music as a nice background creates a solitude for me in the midst of the television and even the sound of dishwashers and washing machines sloshing their way throughout the house.

Headphones? Isn't my point that we need to get away from entertainment? If we listen to music to be entertained, then it's a distraction. But if we listen to music as an aid to worship or as a soothing tone-setter, then it can be a means to a quiet, reflective solitude.

We must get away from responsibilities

We all have obligations. Parents, children, students, teachers, employees or executives, we all have things to do. At times our responsibilities are burdens that weigh us down. At other times they provide satisfying projects that we look forward to. Either way, when we choose to be alone, we need to set them aside for a while. They can wait. If we allow them to preoccupy us, then we are pulled away from being with God. They become ghosts and noisy companions that distract us from the rest and refreshment of solitude.

I find that the way to reduce them for a while is not to deny or suppress them but to give them over to the Lord. I'll touch on this more in chapter 7, when I address learning to settle in God's presence.

Conclusion

Solitude is an issue of relationships. It is also a matter of the heart. We learn to be content to be by ourselves in order to be with God. As we grow in the practice of solitude, our quiet times become quiet. There will be a peace inside, a sense of contentment. Sometimes.

My own experience of solitude is varied. I can be quiet and content for a week or so. Sometimes even longer. But then it changes and I can't let go of the distractions inside me or ignore the demands surrounding me. Then there are times when being alone with God is threatening and painful. I discover that I am feeling the pain of loneliness. Here is a poem that I wrote several years ago:

> I am feeling lonely today,
> as I should be.
> It seems that they have all gone away.
>
> I am feeling lonely.
> But, it's a good loneliness,

A loneliness without threats to myself
Or to those who have left.

Do I have the courage to stay lonely?
Or will I look for quick solutions,
Outward strokes that can't touch the heart,
Time with those with whom I shouldn't be?

I bet if I stay lonely long enough,
It will turn into something else.
I wonder what it will be?

That poem, written in a quiet time, allowed me to face my loneliness and move into solitude. If you have the courage to bring your loneliness to God, he will change it for you too.

GETTING ALONE WITH GOD
Psalm 16:1-11

Approach

Emotionally and mentally step out of all your personal connections; not because they aren't important, but because you want to come back to them strengthened and refreshed from your time alone with God. Make a list of every person with whom you have a connection. Don't rush. Allow yourself time. After you have written down every name you can think of, give the list over to the keeping of the Lord.

In your mind's eye turn now from them to him.

Study

1. Read Psalm 16:1–11. David begins by asking God to make him safe. In what ways does David acknowledge that God has been answering this prayer?

2.   What does it mean to take refuge in God?

3.   Read verses 5 and 6. How do an 'assigned' portion and clear boundary lines contribute to a sense of security?

4.   Read verses 7 and 8. How does David's focus create a sense of safety?

5.   Read verses 9–11. How does David's knowledge of God affect his attitude concerning the end of his life?

Reflection

1.   Spend some time picturing God as a strong fortress surrounding you, providing boundary lines of security. As you do, consider what he is protecting you from and what he is freeing you to do.

2. David has chosen for God and against other gods. Consider what issues, people or concerns compete for your attention and allegiance.

3. David has set the Lord before him. Do that now. Spend time directing your thoughts, emotions, desires, activities and plans towards him. After you have done so, write down how this affects you.

4. David refers to eternal pleasures at God's right hand. Although this looks at life on the other side of death, there are certainly many delightful pleasures from God that we taste now. Think about how you experience 'pleasure in the Lord'.

Prayer

Ask God to teach you how to enjoy him more and find pleasure in his presence.

Ask God to teach you how to order your day so that you can find time on a regular basis to enjoy being with him.

Pray that those you love will find pleasure in the Lord.

CHAPTER 7

FOLLOWING A QUIET TIME PATTERN

Once you have created a quiet place and quiet time, what do you *do* in that quiet time?

Prayer and Bible study are the mainstays of quiet times. In Bible study we seek to hear what God has to say to us. In prayer we speak back to him. In other words, Bible study and prayer are the essential forms of a good spiritual conversation. But we must be careful because the mindset of our age predisposes us to turn almost everything into a technique. While we are doing our Bible study we may somehow lose the conversation, the realization that God is speaking to us, and merely take in information. Or we may just look up a verse or two that gives us a nice thought for the day. We may not use the Bible at all. It is often tempting to do too much too fast and in the wrong way when we approach God, and that's not good. Our approach robs him of his glory and leaves us in spiritual darkness.

If we are going to enjoy our meeting with God first we need to slow down inwardly so that we can relax and open our spiritual eyes and ears. Once we have done that, then we can turn to the Scriptures and feed our souls on God's word. Then, having looked into the Scriptures, we need to look *through* those Scriptures. Like the lenses of spectacles, Scripture will bring into focus the rest of our lives so we can discern our Lord's presence. Having settled into our meeting with God, we are then in a position to pray with spiritual power for ourselves and others.

Warming up and slowing down

At the beginning of a time with God we need to quieten down. Over the years, those who have cultivated a familiar friendship with God have found that there is a need to get settled inwardly or to become 'recollected', as they called it. Martin Luther believed in a period of warming up as we approach God. In his letter, A *Simple Way to Pray, for a Good Friend*, Luther speaks of 'warming the heart', getting the heart to come to itself, waiting until the heart 'gets in the mood'. It is helpful to spend a while in quiet until we find that we want to pray. This takes time.

David knew the necessity of being quiet before God. He writes,

> My heart is not proud, O LORD,
>   my eyes are not haughty;
> I do not concern myself with great matters
>   or things too wonderful for me.
> But I have stilled and quieted my soul;
>   like a weaned child with its mother,
>   like a weaned child is my soul within me.
>   (Psalm 131:1–2)

Being quiet is important if we are to get to know God. Through a prophet he declares,

> Be still, and know that I am God;
>   I will be exalted among the nations,

I will be exalted in the earth.

(Psalm 46:10)

How can we become still – inwardly? First, we mustn't ignore the inner demands and voices. One of the reasons that there is so much noise in our hearts is because we have turned our hearts into a repository of unfinished business. There we dump, store and suppress the pains and emotions that we want to avoid. As soon as we are quiet enough, we can sense all those emotions and concerns clamouring for attention. This is not a comfortable experience. If you try to push them away or keep them down, however, then you will be preoccupied by them and will never be able to become quiet enough for your meeting with God.

The first task in quietening ourselves then is to acknowledge our concerns. As we do that we must give them over to the Lord. There are a number of ways to do this. One way, as I mentioned earlier, is to write out a 'to do' list of pressing issues and then hand it to the Lord. In using this spiritual exercise in situations of spiritual guidance for others I have found that all kinds of things happen when people give the tasks over to the Lord. Not infrequently it is very difficult to let go of the list. We become very attached to our pressing concerns and are threatened to our core when we consider letting them go.

Sometimes I think of myself coming across a cabin in the woods. The cabin has a large veranda with two rocking chairs, one for me, one for the Lord. We sit together looking out at the trees and relaxing. As my concerns come to mind I tell him about them. As

I do, a quiet peace grows inside me. Frequently, but not always, there is a restful stillness that seems to fill the room. I know that this is more than just a mental exercise and that the Lord is really with me there.

When you first begin the process of settling you may feel overwhelmed at the voices and demands. Bear in mind that you may have several years' worth of concerns, feeling and fears stuffed down there. After several months of practising the process of settling it won't always take so long or require so much effort.

After we have stopped being busy inwardly, after we have stopped telling God how to run our lives, and the world, there is a full, resting quiet that we can enter into. When you have reached this stage, you can just sit back and enjoy being with the Lord.

Another reason that it is important to be quiet is so that as we approach our meeting with God we can listen for him. For a couple of years my sons had small personal stereos, which they carried around with them. Theoretically no-one else should have been able to hear the music from the small earphones. The problem came when they wanted to carry on a conversation with me while the earphones were still on. If I spoke to them I had to compete with some rock group pounding away in their ears. So I had a policy: I wouldn't talk until the earphones came off. In our culture, it is as if we have earphones strapped on at birth. The music of the world is always blaring in our ears. The voice of God's Spirit gets drowned out. If we are going to be able to hear with our souls, then we need to get those earphones off!

Listening to God is not just something for the mystic who lives in the desert or for those in Bible times. 'God is always speaking. To hear his voice is not usually a mystical experience . . . To hear him involves no exercise in "tuning in to the right frequency" so much as a humble recognition that it is his prerogative to speak and our responsibility to respond.'[1] Remember the words of Martin Luther quoted in chapter 6, 'I do not know it and do not understand it, but sounding from above and ringing in my ears I hear what is beyond the thought of Man.'[2]

A word of caution. In encouraging you to cultivate an attitude of listening, I am not saying that you should expect to hear an audible voice. You are creating a disposition of expectation and encounter as you seek to meet with God. Joyce Huggett described it this way:

> What I heard in those times of listening was more than a voice. It was a presence. Yes. I heard the Lord call my name. But I also 'heard' his tenderness. I soaked up his love . . . Sometimes it seemed as though Jesus himself stood in front of me or beside me or above me. . . . The only way I can describe it is to liken it to the overwhelming a person feels when they love someone very deeply . . . No words are necessary. They might even be intrusive, for they could trivialize the love.[3]

Reading and study of Scripture

Once we have quietened ourselves, then we are ready to seek to meet God in his word. When our hearts are warm, Scripture becomes the fuel that feeds the spiritual flame of knowledge. However, a proper handling of Scripture requires effort, time and skill. We need to soak in a passage, to read, study and meditate on it, until it becomes a part of us. Jonathan Edwards writes, 'Holy affections are not heat without light . . . knowledge is the key that first opens the hard heart, and enlarges the affections . . .'[4]

Reading the Scriptures as a new Christian was a thrilling and frustrating experience for me. When I opened the book, I sensed on its pages a reality that I knew, yet somehow it seemed just beyond my reach. There were tantalizing tastes, enough to entice me onwards, but something remained elusive. Just as it takes years of education for an engineer to think like an engineer, or a doctor to think like a doctor, so it takes years of soaking in the Scriptures to learn to think like a Christian. The knowledge accumulates with time and effort.

We can't be casual about the Scriptures. Reading a passage from the gospels one day, a couple of verses from Psalms the next, and jumping to the epistles on the next, is not a healthy way to read Scripture. If we study around the Bible rather than studying *it*, reading commentaries and devotionals, listening to teachers in the pulpit, on tapes and on the radio who tell us what the Bible says, we are not really studying the Bible for ourselves. The result is that we lose the direct personal interaction we need with God through the Scriptures.

Step one is reading. It is not difficult: just choose a book of Scripture and read through it. Treat it as you would any book, or perhaps as a letter written to you. Too often we find Scripture to be difficult or obscure because we pick it up, flip to a passage in the middle of say Ephesians or Genesis, read a few verses and then put it down. I can't think of any novel on my shelves that would hold my attention if I treated it that way. Instead, read a book of Scripture from beginning to end. For most New Testament epistles, a complete reading takes less than fifteen minutes. The gospels, Acts or historical books of the Old Testament are much larger, and so take longer. You can take two or three days or more of fifteen to twenty minutes a day to get through a book. Once you know what the whole book is about, then you can go back to favourite passages and read them again. They will make more sense because you know their context.

Step two is to study. I suggested that you read Scripture like a letter written to you, but that's only part of it. You also need to treat Scripture as letters or information written to a family member of several generations ago that have come into your possession. If you are going to make sense of the letters then you need to know something about who wrote them and who they were written to. This requires a bit of investigation.

That great detective Sherlock Holmes is a good model. For several years I tried to get my family to have Sherlock Holmes as a family reading project. It wasn't until we moved to England that everyone became interested, perhaps because then there was a sense of familiarity about it. As we read, we all marvelled at Holmes' ability to pick up clues and come up with what really happened. He walks around asking questions, looks at seemingly insignificant details, and then wanders off to think about it. And, of course, from these seemingly useless titbits of information he is able to solve the crime.

There is a principle of observation involved in Holmes' method. We must look closely at details in our search for clues to the meaning of a book or letter: what problems were being addressed? What needs, fears and concerns did our family members have?

Having looked closely at it, you need to stand back and take it all in. Not only do you have to read a passage several times looking for clues, you have to think about it a lot. Then you can put the pieces together. When you do that you will see the meaning of the book in a way you didn't before. We all have had the experience of struggling to understand something until finally the light of understanding breaks in: 'Of course, now I see what that means!'

Once you have done your work of reading and reflection, it's wise to turn to a reference book. Unless you have had some formal Bible training, you won't know much about, for example, the life of the apostle Paul or the special situations of the churches he was writing to. A good commentary can give that background information. This will further deepen your insight and perhaps correct some erroneous conclusions you may have come to.

Meditating and reflecting

Once you have read and studied a passage, then you are ready to enter into it at a deeper level. Some of the great Bible students after the Reformation used to distinguish between a notional and a real knowledge. Knowing the concepts or the notions is not the same as knowing the spiritual realities that Scripture contains. That is what meditation is all about. We allow ourselves to soak in a passage seeking to have the eyes of our hearts opened. It is not that we see some hidden mystical truth, rather God's truth takes hold of us. God's word and God's Spirit work together to teach us in both mind and heart.

J. I. Packer describes meditation as

> an activity of holy thought, consciously performed in the presence of God, under the eye of God, by the help of God, as a means of communication with God. Its purpose is to clear one's mental and spiritual vision of God and let his truth make its full and proper impact on one's mind and heart.[5]

The book of Psalms is the book of biblical meditation. The first psalm sets the tone and direction for the entire book. It describes the godly person, 'his delight is in the law of the Lord and on his law he meditates day and night' (Psalm 1:2). The rest of the psalms are just that, meditations by David and other godly people of Israel. Sometimes meditation is on the law, precepts and decrees, as in Psalm 119. Other times it is on God's unfailing love (Psalm 48:9), or on his works (Psalm 77:12). But whatever the focus, it takes place in the heart (Psalm 19:14).

Christian meditation differs from Eastern meditation. Whereas Eastern meditation seeks to empty the mind, Christian meditation seeks to focus and fill the mind with the truth of God. Eastern meditation seeks to put aside reason, whereas Christian meditation develops the skilful use of reason, considering the works of God and seeking to understand what they mean. Christian meditation also involves our emotions. We focus on God and his word so much that we feel glad about God's truth, humbled by his law, thrilled with his creation. As can be seen from the Psalms, Christian meditation even combines reflection with emotions in such a way as to produce poetry.

When I choose to meditate on Scripture, or on the love of God, or on the works of God, I find a quiet, secluded place where there are no distractions. For a set period of time I immerse myself in the things of God. Right now I am studying and meditating on Colossians. In the book of Colossians Paul writes of the glorious benefits that we have in Jesus Christ our supreme ascended Lord. Paul calls us to 'Set our minds on things above, not on earthly things' (Colossians 3:2). As I meditate on this, I ponder on what 'things above' and 'earthly things' mean. For heavenly things I consider what life will be like when Jesus comes back, what values of heaven I should be living by in the light of his return, and I long for the rescue from my selfishness, my sinfulness and the circumstances of life that I struggle with while I am waiting. When I finish considering these things, career issues don't seem so urgent and the budget doesn't seem so depressing. I feel uplifted, cleansed and refreshed.

The experience of meditation can be compared with the difference between watching a video and going out to a cinema. The comfortable seats, the large screen, the enveloping sound and the darkened room all help me enter into a story projected on the large screen. Watching a video is enjoyable, but can't compare. People talking, people walking in and out of the room and hopping up to run to the kitchen for a snack are all distractions. I may be watching the same film, but the quality of experience is much more absorbing at the cinema than on video. In the same way, meditating is a more intentional focus on God that leads to a more satisfying encounter with the Truth.

One method of meditation is called *lectio divina*, or 'divine reading'. It means seeking to read Scripture with a heart of devotion in order to be with the Lord. Basil Pennington describes it this way:

> It is not a question of reading a paragraph, a page or a chapter. It is, rather, sitting down with a friend, the Lord, and letting him speak to us. We listen. And if what he says in the first word or the first sentence strikes us, we stop and let it sink in. We relish it. We respond from our heart. We enjoy it to the full before we move on. There is no hurry. We are sitting with our friend . . . We let him speak. We really listen.[6]

As you read, there will be times when you will have a sense of being nourished in your heart.

Certain passages will seem to strike home. The disciples on the road to Emmaus experienced that on the resurrection day. As they walked with Jesus he explained how the Old Testament required his death and resurrection. After Jesus left them they commented, 'Were not our hearts burning within us while he talked with us on the road and opened the Scriptures to us?' (Luke 24:31–32).

This experience is wonderful when it happens, but it won't always happen in our quiet time. We can look for it, we can expect it, but we can't require it or demand it. Sometimes you will just be gaining information. That's fine. Keep in mind that Scripture is the vocabulary of the Spirit. During the day passages of Scripture that you have read previously may come to mind and bring the wisdom or spiritual nurture you need for your specific situation.

Some people find it helpful to use their imagination for biblical meditation. It is wise to be cautious about this, but from time to time it may be beneficial. My experience with it in the context of discipling others is that it has proved to be powerful and enlightening. Once I was having a quiet time with a new friend who was very active in our church. We were studying Psalm 1, which is about the value of meditating on Scripture. During his quiet time, Bill pictured himself as a tree growing his roots by a river. He was shocked, however, when his tree fell over and into the river. As we discussed what this might mean, it seemed to suggest that he was so busy doing things for the Lord that he had not taken time to become rooted in Scripture.

Meditation is not limited to the Scriptures because God's word is not limited to the Scriptures. Tozer comments, 'The Bible will never be a living book to us until we are convinced that God is articulate in His universe.'[7] God speaks to us in a variety of ways. I think it is especially important to pay attention to the events and experiences of our lives. If we choose to listen and look we may sometimes be able to discern him there. I find that if I consider the experiences of my life reflectively, pay attention to my emotional responses and ask how I see God's hand, I frequently get spiritual insights and direction.

There is a spiritual exercise for this type of reflection that I use for myself and in spiritual guidance for others. I make three columns on a page and title them 'Experiences', 'Emotions' and 'Perceptions'. It looks like this:

Experiences	Emotions	Perceptions

In the 'Experiences' column list *events* and *experiences* or *major issues*. It will not matter if these things happened yesterday, in the past week, or in the course of the last year. Each time you change the focus you will discover new insights about God's work. Your list doesn't have to be in any special order. Nor do you need to write them out in complete sentences. Just use one or two words that remind you of things you can recall. Don't look for things that are necessarily 'spiritual', as all your experiences and concerns are worthy of consideration.

The 'Emotions' column is for your emotional responses to each event listed in the first column. In just a word or two write down your emotions as you can recall them ('satisfied', 'disappointed', 'pleased', 'upset' and so on). It is important that you pay attention to your emotions. They are tools that help you discern what is going on in your heart. I will talk about this more in the next chapter.

The 'Perceptions' column is to help you reflect on what God is doing in your life. Look over all that you have written in the 'Experiences' and 'Emotions' columns, and see if you can identify ways that God has been working. Do you see any common themes or patterns? Is there an inner conviction that God has been working in you or through you?

As you consider your perceptions remember that God requires us to respond to him. It may be that as you look at your week you will see that you are frequently in situations in which you are having to ask forgiveness of others. In this case it may be that God is calling you to practise humility. Or it may be that you are confronted with a series of crises in which others were let down by you. Perhaps, then, God is requiring you to be more responsible to others.

Praying

Having spent time with God in quiet and in Scripture, you are now in a position to pray with spiritual wisdom and power. Biblical prayer comes from hearts that have life by the Spirit, are shaped by the Scriptures and are enriched by meditation.

Prayer is very simple, but amazingly difficult. It is something a newborn believer in Christ can do from the very first. Yet it is also something that the greatest saints must still struggle through. It requires a life-long effort. It also can be confusing and threatening. A thousand questions come to mind, plus objections, reservations, hesitations. How should we approach God? What should we say? How should we say it? What right do we have to ask God for anything? How do we know that he will answer? How can the eternal God listen to our small concerns?

Broadly conceived prayer can be thought of as communion with God. This is what you do in your quiet time from beginning to end. But there is also a narrow focus which can be expressed as 'asking God for help'. What is difficult about that? You just tell God what you need. That is not very easy to do, however. When I pray, I admit that I face problems that are beyond me. I am acknowledging that God is God and I am not. Life is bigger than me and I need his help.

Look through the prayers of the Bible where people are doing business with God: Abraham seeking a son, David crying out for deliverance from his enemies, Nehemiah asking for help in rebuilding

Jerusalem, and so on. God's people come to him with problems or needs and ask for help. But that is why it is so hard and will always be so.

Once we have come to terms with our limits, and are willing to pray out of our need, then as Christians we need to keep in mind that we are to pray in Jesus' name. Jesus told the disciples, 'You may ask me for anything in my name, and I will do it' (John 14:14). To pray in this way is much more than slapping the liturgical formula 'in Jesus' name, Amen' to the end of our prayers.

What does this mean? To understand it properly, we need to put Jesus' teaching in context. He was sending the disciples out, their training being almost over. It was the night before his crucifixion. The disciples felt the weight of the moment and were overwhelmed. How could they carry on without Jesus? The assuring answer was prayer. For the work to which Jesus assigned them, they could ask for what they needed and be assured that they would receive it. The condition was that they had to ask in Jesus' name. That is, they had to ask with the concern and commitment to do Jesus' work and to fulfil his commission.

For you and I to pray in Jesus' name means that we too join in the mission. We are making a commitment to do what Jesus wants Christians to do until he returns. So before we pray we must ask ourselves if we are part of his team. Do our motives align with his kingdom? This way of praying transforms us. It reshapes our thinking about ourselves and all of life. It turns us away from self-centredness. We don't serve ourselves, we serve the Lord.

I don't think this means that we have to be missionaries, ministers or in 'full-time Christian service'. We can ask for our personal needs too, as the kingdom of God is much broader than our traditional understanding of ministry. But we must be careful here. Even when we ask for personal needs, we must bear in mind that the whole focus of our lives is not personal gratification but is obedience to the will of our Lord. Jesus prayed in the Garden of Gethsemane, 'not my will but yours be done' (Luke 22:42). The issue is submitting our lives to Christ and living and praying under his Lordship.

When we pray, it is helpful to use a list. There is an old saying: 'Aim at nothing and you are sure to hit it.' If we don't have a list, our prayers will probably be wandering, unfocused and haphazard. I am not particularly disciplined and so developing a prayer list for daily use is something I tend to avoid. There are times when I don't use one. But I am using one currently and experiencing some very satisfying times of intercession. Despite my fears of getting caught in empty religious repetition, I am convinced that a list is the best way to go about regular prayers. Simply opening my notebook with my prayer list and placing it on my desk helps me be settled and consistent. And there is something about it that focuses my wandering thoughts. Through the daily practice of using it, my whole being knows it's time to settle down and do business with God.

A prayer list can be as sophisticated as index cards with pictures of people you pray for, or it can be a simple sheet of paper that you have jotted words on. The first couple of pages in the front of my journal is where I write the names of people I am praying for or a brief description of issues I am concerned about. As my prayers are answered, I put a mark and a date by my request. Your faith will grow as you see answers and begin crossing things off your list. God answers prayers all the time, but we often miss this because we aren't looking. When you pray daily and keep a list, you will be much more inclined to recognize answers when they come.

Additionally, as you pray you will find that your prayers become sharpened. As I pray through my list of friends, I start off generally asking God's blessing. But over the weeks I learn about problems at home, a deep hurt from years past, or a major crisis at work, that all need God's help. And as I pray with more insight for needs, there is a growing experience of God's loving power.

There are two extremes to avoid in making a list. You don't want it to be too general or too specific. We can sweep over issues for prayer with a broad wave, 'God, please help my friend, Bill,' or 'Please help me to do better today.' Such prayers can be a mere attempt to do our religious duty without extending ourselves or engaging God.

But not all general prayers are bad. The Lord's Prayer is a prayer list that is quite broad. The petitions are brief and cover all our basic needs in just a few sentences. The clear simplicity of them helps us focus on what is essential.

We also need to pray specifically. The general needs covered in the Lord's Prayer express themselves in our lives in specific ways. Our need for daily bread may be expressed in balancing our bank account or seeking a pay rise. Forgiveness of sins may mean asking for forgiveness for harbouring anger towards your spouse or friend. Deliverance from temptation may require keeping a chaste attitude towards someone at work or not cheating on the expense account.

Taking your cues from the Lord's Prayer, your specific requests need not be detailed. Tell God what you want. Don't say it repeatedly. Don't elaborate. Just tell him. Pray for one entry on your list, then move on to the next. But be careful as you pray. In contrast to being too general, we can become so specific that we clutter our prayers and cloud up what we are really seeking from God. Jesus cautions against this when he says that we should not pray like the pagans who think they will be heard because of their many words (Matthew 8:8). He instructs us that God knows what we need before we even ask. Our prayers are to seek his help, not to inform him or manipulate him.

Praying also requires persistence. Praying for something once is seldom enough. We must pray repeatedly until we sense that God says no, or until he answers our prayer. We may think that speaking to God about something once is enough. After all, God knows our needs anyway. Or, for something bigger, we hope that perhaps mentioning our concerns to him a couple of times a week will do the trick. But over the years I have discovered that it is the things that I repeatedly call out to the Lord for on a daily basis which get answers. It makes sense when you think about it. One of God's requirements for prayer is a sense of need. If we are not interested enough to call out to God on a daily basis, then we must not be very needy. In that case we can't expect him to take us too seriously.

Finally, I want to emphasize that those who pray must learn to wait. Sometimes we must wait for months. Sometimes we must wait for years. What must it have been like for Zechariah, the father of John the Baptist, when the angel showed up in the temple and announced that his prayers had been answered? 'Do not be afraid, Zechariah; your prayer has been heard. Your wife Elizabeth will bear you a son, and you are to give him the name John' (Luke 1:13). By the time the angel showed up Zechariah and Elizabeth were very old, far beyond the child-bearing years. Surely they had given up praying for children a long time ago. Zechariah must have wondered, 'What prayers?'

Waiting on the Lord takes us to the heart of prayer. When we wait, we are reminded that God works according to his time, not our convenience. When we wait, we are placed in a position of humility. Waiting puts us in the right place before God, longing for him to hear us and respond.

Prayer is hard work. But God not only meets our needs as we wait, he also gives us refreshment of body and soul. Isaiah writes, 'They that wait upon the Lord will renew their strength. They will soar on wings like eagles; they will run and not grow weary, they will walk and not be faint' (Isaiah 40:31). When I sit quietly and expectantly before the Lord in prayer, frequently I sense the room filled with a restoring fullness that is cleansing and renewing.

Putting it all together

Here is how these elements of a quiet time fit together.

```
┌─────────────────────────────────────────┐
│                  Prayer                  │
└─────────────────────────────────────────┘

 ┌───────────────────────────────────────┐
 │     Meditating and reflecting on life   │
 └───────────────────────────────────────┘

 ┌───────────────────────────────────────┐
 │       Study and reading God's Word      │
 └───────────────────────────────────────┘

┌─────────────────────────────────────────┐
│             Warming up to God            │
└─────────────────────────────────────────┘
```

How long will all this take? It could take an hour or more if you wanted it to, but it can be done in twenty-five or thirty minutes. You could spend six or seven minutes slowing down, ten minutes in Scripture reading and study, five or so minutes in meditation and five minutes in prayer.

The goal is balance. You probably won't use all four elements every day. On one day you may spend most of your quiet time in settling and reading Scripture, and on the next you may meditate through a passage and then pray. Over the course of a month or two, we need to spend time in warming up our hearts, time in study and meditation and time in prayer.

Keep in mind as well that to focus on one element for an extended period is not healthy. It shouldn't be all Bible study, or all prayer, or all getting settled. Imagine eating only steak for two months, or only fruit. It wouldn't be long before we would notice physical (and perhaps mental) health problems. You should seek to create a sense of variety. And although there will be times when it seems a duty, that should not be the norm for your quiet time. Meeting God should never be humdrum and boring. Through it all there should be expectation, excitement and desire.

SECURITY IN THE LORD

Psalm 30:6–12

Occasionally, I experience what I call the 'jerked rug' phenomena. It seems to come when I am feeling pretty good about myself, a bit too good. When the rug gets pulled and I stumble, I find that I am not quite as clever or as wise as I wanted to believe.

Over the years I have come to appreciate these experiences as gifts from God. If he allowed me to continue in my own self-generating confidence, pride would become a hardened shell around my heart. But when the pressures of life become greater than I can handle, I am forced to face my own limitations. It is during those times that I experience anew the wonderful grace of a God who is there to give security far beyond my own capacity.

Approach

Have you ever had a cupboard so full of clutter that you were afraid to open it? Often our hearts are like cupboards where we throw in unwanted feelings and unsatisfied desires. After a while, we don't want to open the door because all those unpleasant things will fall out and make a mess. The problem is, if our hearts are cluttered, the spiritual and emotional dimension of life is lost.

Take some time now to open up your heart. Allow things to fall out. Over the course of this study you will be asking God to help you clean it up. Write down whatever desires, hurts and concerns you may find.

After you have done that sit in quiet anticipation of what God will do.

Study

1. Read Psalm 30:6–12. How would you describe David's relationship with God (verses 6–7)?

2. What reasons does David present to God in favour of his deliverance (verses 9–10)?

3. Look over the entire psalm. Now how would you describe David's relationship with God?

Reflect and meditate

1. Difficult circumstances can cause us to reflect on the character of God. How have the circumstances of your life affected your relationship with God?

2. David expresses some of the ups and downs of his life. Consider the last six to twelve months of your life and then chart your ups and downs.

	1	2	3	4	5	6
Ups						
Downs						

3. Meditate through the ups and downs, picturing the Lord with you through each phase. Once you have done that, write down your insights and emotions.

Prayer

Ask God to give you the courage to face the unpleasant experiences of life that may be important but unresolved.

Ask God to give the members of your church the courage to face conflicts that need to be dealt with.

Ask God to bring the nations to face the unpleasant experiences of life that are important and producing conflict.

CHAPTER 8
QUIET TIME
COMPANIONS

One of the best ways to enhance our spiritual growth is to share our quiet time with at least one friend – a quiet time companion. Spiritual growth requires that we spend time alone. But this does not mean we grow in isolation. Once we have spent time alone with God we need to be able to spend time with other believers.

Having a quiet time companion has a number of benefits. For one thing, it helps us to talk about God. In many Christian gatherings God is an assumed presence. We gather in his name. We come together to do his work. We sing songs about him, we pray to him. But what do we say to each other when we want to talk about him and his work in our lives? It seems that we often talk around him. However, when we have a friend with whom we share our quiet times, God becomes the direct object of our conversations.

Sharing our quiet times with a quiet time companion enhances our spiritual discernment. We may not be aware that God is working in some area of our lives until we begin to talk about it. Perhaps we feel deserted as we face a problem at work or at home. However, as we articulate our frustrations about our sense of his absence to a friend, we may realize that the problems themselves are a means of facing an inner struggle that we had been avoiding.

Sharing our quiet times can protect us from error. We may think God is calling or directing us in some way, but then perhaps we are deceiving ourselves? As we share our hesitations and concerns a friend can help us explore that sense of leading and compare it with God's word in the Scriptures.

Guidelines

How do you find a friend with whom to share your quiet time? What issues should you consider?

First, within your church or Christian fellowship look for someone who displays a hunger for God. A good indicator is whether he or she attends regularly. The chances are they are coming because there is some spiritual drive. Look as well for someone at work who shows signs of having some spiritual life. If they are willing to be open about their faith at work it's likely that they are pursuing God.

You will want to find someone on your spiritual level. If you look for someone older and more experienced than you, or perhaps not as mature as you, then sharing your quiet times can turn into a discipling relationship. This can inhibit openness and spiritual intimacy as you move into a one up/one down situation. While talking about a quiet time can be an effective discipling tool, it needs to be clear from the start that you are involved in discipling, not a spiritual friendship.

It is also necessary that you consider whether your potential quiet time companion is trustworthy. You will be sharing some very intimate information. You need to know that your friend won't use it against you or tell others. Trust is something that grows over time. The first few times you meet together you may want to share in general terms. As trust is built up, you can share more of what you are learning about God and what he is doing inside your heart.

What do you do when you meet together?

First it must be clear that everything you say will be confidential. You must both agree that nothing will be said beyond the meeting without permission; not even as a prayer request to a few 'trusted' others.

Secondly, agree on when, where and for how long you will meet. You will need at least an hour if you are both going to share. If there is time it is helpful to spend a while in quiet worship and prayer as well. You should also set an initial limit for the number of meetings you plan to have. Six weeks is a good time frame. If things don't work out, then you can easily stop them. If you find that meeting together is mutually beneficial, then you can extend it for another two or three months, after which you can evaluate again.

Next you need to agree that the purpose of your meeting together is specifically to talk about your quiet times. Do this, not because other areas of your lives are not important, but because it is so easy to get distracted. If you are not careful you will end up talking about anything but God and your quiet times. In one of my spiritual friendships we intended to talk about our prayer lives but by the third meeting we were discussing theological and philosophical ideas. In another we started out talking about God and ended up sharing the struggles we were having in our professions and in raising our children.. In both cases the discussions were stimulating and helpful, but they were distractions nevertheless. And in both cases, we never did seem to get back to focusing on quiet times.

As to a procedure, there is no single right way. Experiment to see what works best. Allow one person to share all the way through the elements and dynamics of his or her quiet time and then let the other share. Another time have one person talk about one part of his or her quiet time and then the other can share the same elements and dynamics as well.

While one person shares, the role of the other is to listen and clarify with an accepting attitude. Never criticize, correct or counsel. The role of the listener is to be gracious, welcoming and affirming. Keep in mind that you are not there to psychoanalyse each other, counsel each other or solve each other's problems. Your goal is to talk about what is happening in your quiet times. As you do, God may do some deep work, but you must leave that to him.

The partner who listens must have two goals in mind. One goal is to listen and ask questions in a way that will help your partner discern what the Lord may be doing and saying. The other goal is to help your partner express how he or she is responding to God's action in his or her life. Although we might like to think that we are eager to respond in willing obedience, often our response is resistance. We may tell ourselves that we are open when in fact we are not. By having your partner ask how you are feeling about God's work in your life, such acts of resistance can be exposed. When that happens, you are in a position to tell God honestly how you feel. This opens up channels of communication. If you don't face your resistance your quiet time can become a mere formality and dry up.

As we share with a partner we need to keep asking each other, is there a sense of meeting with God? Or do I just feel like I am going through the motions? By sharing from the quiet time pattern in chapter 7, we can begin to open up to each other and develop the quality of our time with God.

What to talk about

When we explore our attempts to get quiet with a friend, we open up all kinds of spiritual dynamics that yield helpful insights. Questions that we can ask each other include: Are we able to get quiet? What is the tone or feel of our quiet? Is there a pull towards God or a dull, lifeless silence? Are we able to give our concerns over to God or do we cling to them and allow them to gnaw at us?

As we talk about our experience of settling in his presence, we may find that we are holding tight to something and can't let it go. Perhaps for a student there is an anxiety about an imminent exam. No matter how much she tries, she can't seem to turn it over to the Lord. Or perhaps a mother continually worries about one of her children in school. Even after much prayer the anxiety is still strong. Perhaps a businessman can't seem to turn over his concerns for year-end profits.

It may be such struggles will indicate areas of our lives that have not yet been brought under the Lordship of Christ. Or it may be that we have a hurt or fear from the past that we don't even remember. The mother may have forgotten that a friend from her childhood was hurt. Inwardly she wonders if God can be trusted for her child now since her friend was hurt then. For the student struggling with exam preparation, the real problem may be a fear of letting down her parents. Or perhaps it is a fear that her future career may somehow be damaged. Upon exploration the businessman may discover he can't turn over his concern for profits because he has overspent his income for some new addition on his house. In prayer he needs to face his stewardship of his resources. As these root causes come out in discussion, it is then possible to begin to pray about them and see specific results.

It may be that when we seek to get quiet we experience only a sense of deadness. As we talk about this with a friend it may become clear that there is buried anger we didn't even know about. Once we have uncovered our anger we can tell God about it, seek guidance about a proper response and move on. The task in all these is to bring them to the Lord. As we give over the pain of the past, we may not see an immediate answer or solution, but there will be freedom to trust him for the anxieties of the present and the future.

In sharing what happens in our settling time, we can evaluate our sense of heart. Although emotions vary, they can be placed on a scale ranging from the very positive to the completely negative. On the positive side is a sense of gratitude, an inner spontaneous sense of thanks that rises from within. This is the work of the Spirit that cries 'Abba, Father' within us. Such a response is a pleasant indicator of spiritual health. At the other extreme, we can have a sense of deadness. As we try to become quiet there is no response inside. If this is experienced consistently over a period of time there may be some sort of blockage that needs to be explored. Between gratitude and nothing is a sense of turbulence. Anxieties and fears experienced in our quiet time mean that our hearts are alive to God but that there are issues to be worked through. The task is to pay attention to this emotional turbulence and ask God what is going on.

We can expect to move back and forth in our quiet times. Any one stage experienced for extended periods needs to be evaluated. A prevailing sense of thankfulness with a constantly cheery attitude can be an indicator that we are avoiding something that we don't want to face or bring to God.

Gratitude	Turbulence	Nothing

Sharing about Bible study

As we share about our quiet times we can also explore what is happening when we study and meditate on Scripture. Questions that quiet time companions can ask each other include: What new insight or knowledge did you glean about God? What seemed to strike your heart in a new way? What seemed to apply to your immediate situation? What do you think God was asking you to do?

Sharing of our personal discoveries in Scripture can be especially encouraging for both partners. Shared insights tend to feed on each other. On hearing my friend talk about the benefits of perseverance, say from Romans 5, I may experience new insights. My struggles may take on a new meaning as I am reminded that God uses such struggles to work patience into my character. Or it may be that my study of Scripture did not seem particularly nourishing. However, when I talk about what I didn't seem to learn something clicks into place. Like a spark between us I see what God has been saying all along but I hadn't heard up until that point.

When we talk about Scripture, we want to be sure that we are paying attention to what God has spoken through the authors of Scripture. That is, we will want to be able to say what we think God was saying in the original situation. On the other hand, we want to be able to express what we think God is saying to us now as well.

One of the benefits of sharing study and insights is that we can hold each other accountable. It may be that what my friend is saying about a passage is inspiring but doesn't seem to make sense as I read over it. In that case, it is important to ask for further clarification. If I just can't see it, then I must say so. Too often we treat Scripture as putty that we shape to mean what we want it to. As spiritual partners we can help each other cope with and confront this temptation.

On the other hand, it may be that week after week my friend goes into great detail about what he is learning from his study. It all sounds great and really he does get some meaty insights. Somewhere along the way, however, I begin to notice that he seldom or never talks about how God is speaking to him in his present situation from Scripture. It is appropriate to point this out and ask if he may somehow be avoiding God.

Sharing about times of reflection

The exercise of listing experiences, emotions and perceptions can help in sharing our reflections. Talking to another person about what has happened over the past week or so and how we felt about it, can help us begin to discern any recurring responses, or patterns hinting at how God has been working.

Once I was sharing from my perceptions column (see chapter 7) about God's working in my life. It was frustrating and felt as if nothing was working out to my expectations. As I talked about this with my friend, he wondered if God was asking me to give up a sense of control. We explored what this might mean and it seemed that God was asking me to 'let go'. At that point it was not clear exactly what I was supposed to let go of, or how I was to go about doing so. However, over the next few months, it became clear that some ministry programmes in the church needed radical changes. Changing them was hard, but not as hard as it could have been. I had already been warned. I knew that God was involved in shaping the ministry programmes for his purposes and I could let go by allowing them to change.

Sharing about prayer

Finally quiet time companions can ask each other how their prayers are going. Questions we can ask each other include: Who do you feel especially called to pray for? Do you have a sense that God is hearing your prayers? What answers to prayers have you received recently? What do you find difficult to pray about?

As we talk about our prayers with a friend we can begin to see ways that God is leading us in our prayers and sharpening them. Our prayers for others can start out with a general request such as, 'God please help Bob in his job,' or 'Please help Bill deal with the discipline problems at home.' As we pray we may find that we get insight on how to pray for Bob's work situation or what to ask specifically for Bill as he seeks to set godly limits with his son. Talking about our sense of leading in prayer with another can sharpen and clarify just how God is leading us.

When we talk about our prayers with a friend, we can begin to discern areas of our own prayer life that need more attention. At one point I was struggling with my sense of calling. God seemed to be asking me to move on to another ministry. However, I found it very difficult to pray about what I should do. When I shared this struggle, I discovered that there was some unresolved pain with a couple of colleagues. Before I could pray freely about my future, I had to face the relational issues of the past and present.

When we talk about our prayers with a quiet time companion, we will want to consider our level of conviction, compassion and consistency. When we pray with conviction, we have an awareness of the importance of the issue. There is a sense of gravity about it. When we pray with compassion there is a shared emotion, we can feel with the people we are praying for. When we pray with consistency there is a regular pattern to our prayers, it's something that we want to pray about on a daily basis. If our prayers for someone or some issue lack conviction, compassion and consistency, it may be that we are not being called to carry that person or issue in prayer, or it may be that we need to take a closer look at our times of intercession.

As we share our prayers with a friend, our faith that God answers prayers will grow. We have a mutual mission, we are seeking God's kingdom and working together to see his will is done on earth the way that it is done in heaven. Nothing can be more exciting and fulfilling than this.

Having a quiet time together

We don't need to stop at talking about our quiet times, we can also sometimes have a quiet time together. Initially this may seem strange, two people sitting in a room being quiet for twenty or thirty minutes. However, it can be extremely powerful. There is something enriching about the shared silence. Many times I find the room is filled with the Lord's presence in a warm, full quiet that is often tender and affectionate. I used to think this was my imagination, but I soon discovered that more often than not my partner had the same sense of presence.

What do you do when you have a quiet time together? After a period of being quiet, in which you have had time to settle, look at Scripture and pray, share what has happened. Working through the same process together as you do individually brings an immediacy and a freshness to your devotions and to your sharing. Instead of talking about quiet times over the past week or two, you are sharing about what happened in the past fifteen or twenty minutes.

In sharing a quiet time and meeting to talk about our quiet times we confront the forces of spiritual darkness in a significant way. As we meet to talk about God, we are directly challenging the secularized mindset that we have inherited from our culture. Remember that we have been socialized not to speak about God in public. Having formed this habit of sanitizing our language of spiritual things in public, we tend to do so in our private lives and in our Christian gatherings. However, as we talk about what has been happening when we meet with God, we learn to recognize his presence. In this way we open up our spiritual eyes and reverse the process of God-blindness. We begin to repair the rods and cones of our spiritual eyes. God becomes more than someone we know about. We are knowing him in our personal experience and through the experience of our quiet time companion. As we have quiet times in which we meet with God, not only do we learn to be with him but we also learn to see and hear him in all his world.

Here are some questions you might like to use when meeting with your quiet time companion.

Settling down and warming up	*Are we able to get quiet?*
	What is the tone or feel of our quiet?
	Is there a pull towards God or a dull, lifeless silence?
	Are we able to give our concerns over to God or do we cling to them and allow them to gnaw at us?
Reading and study	*What new information are we learning about God?*
	What seemed to strike our hearts in a new way?
	What seemed to apply to our immediate situation?
	What do we think that God may be asking us to do?
Reflection and meditation	*How do we see God working in our lives?*
	What may God be saying to us through our experiences?
	What may God be asking us to do in and through our circumstances?
Prayer	*Who do we feel especially called to pray for?*
	Do we have a sense that God is hearing our prayers?
	What answers to prayers have we

received recently?

What do we find difficult to pray about?

Are we able to ask for help?

Overall issues

Do we have a sense of meeting with God?

How are we responding to God?

What may the Lord be saying to us?

WE ARE CHOSEN

Approach

We all have needs. Our needs can get in the way of knowing God, or they can be a means of getting to know him better. Step one in spiritual growth is knowing what our needs are. Step two is knowing how to give them to God so that he can aid us. Begin to approach God by asking him to bring your needs to mind. Write down every one that you can think of. As you write them down, ask God to shoulder the burden with you.

Introduction

In a seminar on prayer I asked participants to chart their lives on a large sheet of paper. On their chart they were to illustrate the role of prayer in their lives.

When people shared their charts a couple of themes emerged. For most, prayer was more prevalent in the ups and downs of life and not so much during the plateaux in between. We also saw that for most, prayer sprang from a response to God's help in hard times. It wasn't so much that people prayed and God answered, as God helped and then we started to ask for it.

Does that seem strange to you? It was to me, until I thought about it in the light of the Scriptures. In common with all religions, Christianity shares a belief in a divine being that should be worshipped. There the similarity ends, however. In other religions the divine being is pursued in order to receive aid for the traumas of life. In Ephesians the apostle Paul helps us to see that the real nature of God is to seek us out before it even occurs to us that we need him.

Study

1. Read Ephesians 1:1–6. Paul refers to Jesus Christ in each of the three lines of his salutation (verses 1–2). Read over these verses several times. From Paul's greeting what can you discern about the apostle Paul, the Ephesians and God?

2. God the Father is the subject of praise in verses 3 and 6. Re-read these verses several times as well. How would you describe Paul's attitude towards God?

3. Paul's enthusiasm comes from what God has done for us in Jesus Christ. According to Paul in verses 3–5, what specific results come into the life of a Christian because we are chosen and loved by God?

4. What are the roles of the Father and of Jesus Christ in bringing us these benefits?

The Father	Jesus Christ

Reflection

1. In verse 3 Paul writes that 'we have every spiritual blessing in the heavenly realms'. Imagine that you have made it through life all the way to heaven and you are safely inside. How do you think it will feel?

2. In Christ you are assured of that eternal safety. What difference can it make in the way you live now to know that?

3. The first spiritual blessing Paul mentions is that we are chosen by God. Think about a time when you were chosen for a task or given a special honour. How did it affect you?

How much more of a privilege it is to be chosen by God! Picture yourself in a crowd at a beach. As you are standing there Jesus comes along and invites you to follow him. How do you respond? What anticipations and reservations do you experience?

CHAPTER 9
QUIET TIME DYNAMICS

Once I went for eight months without a quiet time. It was not a good time in my life. But it was a spiritually powerful time. My relationship with God was reflected in my quiet time, or rather, my lack of one. During that time I was spiritually nurtured by worship services and Christian friends. More than once I struggled with feelings of guilt. I felt that I should be having quiet times but just couldn't bring myself around.

Before this dry spell, I had set aside several hours a day for a number of months to seek the Lord. Again and again I had called out to him to change me. When he began to answer my prayers, it was not what I was expecting. Not only my quiet times, but all of my life was shaken and transformed by God's work. It was a confusing period in my life and I coped by avoiding quiet times altogether. God didn't reject me during that time. When I was able to begin again, he was there with a warm welcome and affirmation.

Quiet times go through shifting phases because all that happens in our lives with God is connected with a quiet time. I have found that at times they are regular and consistent. At times they are rich and sweet; other times, dry and boring. This diversity of experience no longer surprises me. My quiet times vary widely because the work of God's Spirit in my life varies widely. Initially I felt guilty about these ebbs and flows. I don't anymore. Knowing God, like knowing any other person, is an ever-changing experience.

Using your emotions

Whenever we sit down to be with God, our emotions are affected. God is a person. Just like any other personal relationship, knowing him involves emotions. With my emotions I sense his care for me, embrace his word, and, I must confess, react to his commands.

This idea may invite some controversy. Talking about emotions among Christians can be, well, emotional. Some pride themselves on their reserve. Others take pride in their ability to express what is on their hearts. For those who value restraint, let me say that I am not here advocating indulging in outward displays of feeling. For those who have found great benefit in the emotional side of faith, you should remember that emotions are natural responses that vary from time to time and should not be forced or manipulated.

Both in the Bible, and in history, we see godly people whose emotions were central to their encounters with God. As the Psalms testify, David experienced tremendous heights and great depths throughout his life. Elijah, Jeremiah, Jonah, Habakkuk, to mention but a few, all had their ups and (lots of) downs.

Can we see emotions as helpful indicators of the spiritual life within? Do we stop to think that our down times may be more than mere depression and are perhaps a sign of spiritual need?

Jonathan Edwards used the term 'religious affections' to describe our emotional response to God, and regarded emotions as a means of spiritual insight. Edwards wrote of 'a sense of heart wherein the mind not only speculates and beholds, but relishes and feels'.

During the first Great Awakening in New England, when critics wanted to dismiss the revival as nothing more than an excess of emotions, Jonathan Edwards defended it, saying that God was not interested in mildly affected worshippers. In fact, Edwards turned the table on those who were upset by all the emotional displays. He demonstrated that in Scripture the worst possible spiritual state was a hard and unaffected heart. What God desires is for our hearts to burn with a desire for him.

Edwards also pointed out that spiritual affections are not merely 'emotional highs'. We also experience times of grief and mourning as we draw close to God and discover our need to be cleansed and purified.

A word of caution; strong emotions are not a guarantee that God's Spirit is at work. Satan can duplicate almost anything. The way to discern true spiritual affection is in our love for God. Are we growing in affectionate appreciation of him: his might, majesty and beauty? And when we are emotionally down are we in self-pity or are we reaching out to seek God's consolation?

No matter how spiritually mature we become, we never outgrow our emotions. When I was a new believer, I experienced great emotional swings which

I was told would level out as I approached spiritual maturity. I kept waiting for my ups and downs to die away. But after being a Christian leader in college, four years of theological training and a good number of years in ministry, my swings weren't levelling out like they were supposed to do. My ups and downs weren't as unsettling as time went on (for a start, I stopped fearing that God had left me). But, if anything, my feelings were more intense. I began to worry about my apparent spiritual immaturity. When was I going to grow up? Eventually I learned that, because my relationship with God is a personal encounter, I must give myself permission to feel; both the ups and the downs.

Once we are open to our emotions before the Lord, fresh springs of spiritual life can well up. And there is no better place to embrace our emotions, our spiritual affections, than in our quiet times.

Quiet time phases

I have noticed at least five distinct phases in my devotional life, and I call them: occasional quiet time, determined quiet time, study quiet time, desert quiet time and devotional quiet time.

Each phase is a reflection of spiritual movements in my life with God. Each phase has its own characteristics and feel, each has its own strengths and weaknesses, its own dangers and delights. The first two phases mentioned, the occasional and determined quiet times, are characterized by their frequency, by how often we have a quiet time. The study quiet time focuses on what we do in our meeting with God. The desert and devotional quiet times are distinguished by how we feel as we meet with God.

How we grow through the phases of our quiet times depends on how God is working in us. This is why it is not good to be judgmental of yourself or others, about which phase you are in. There is no formula for how to do it. We should not expect to move through the phases in order. Nor should we expect to experience every phase.

Let's consider the stages of our devotional life in more detail. We can get a picture of what each one is like as we look at our use of Scripture, prayer, our emotions, frequency, our sense of the Lord's presence and our reasons for practising quiet times as a spiritual discipline.

Occasional quiet time

When you are in the occasional quiet time phase, you have no regular discipline of meeting with the Lord. Time set aside with the Lord is not a focus or priority, so Scripture reading tends to be the 'skip and dip' method. You pick up the Bible whenever you feel the need and read wherever it falls open. (My tendency is to end up in the Psalms when I slip into this phase.) It is a bit like eating on the run; you grab a sandwich, an apple or a biscuit as you rush through the kitchen and out the back door.

In the occasional phase prayer tends to be haphazard and task-oriented. I pray only when there is a need. It's usually some version of 'Lord, help me with this', or, 'Lord, please do that'. For the most part, even when I do sit down to be with the Lord, there is little sense of worship. I am usually so busy inside from my continuous running, that I can't hear (and join) the Spirit as he cries 'Abba, Father' within me.

My emotional response to the Lord is erratic. Sometimes I am excited about him, other times I am not. Most of the time, in this phase of my life, there are things other than God consciously on my mind and heart.

Although the occasional phase is something most of us go through, it is not a good place to be for very long. God is moved to the edge of our lives rather than the centre where he belongs. Usually there is no intention to be so casual with God, it just seems to happen. Despite good intentions to set aside time with God, it seems like there is just too much to do. There is always one more phone call to make, or one more page to read, or one more urgent meeting to attend. Somehow God is moved aside in the rush of our busy schedules.

If you have spent very long having quiet times only occasionally, then you need to set your heart to meet with the Lord daily. You will need to be firm about it and guard your time. Don't let anything get in the way until you are established in it.

Determined quiet time

The determined quiet time phase is the opposite to the occasional phase. It is when you have a time with God every day, without fail. Whereas in the occasional phase, your quiet time comes and goes depending on how you feel, the determined quiet time is practised regardless of how you feel. You set aside time each day, and each day at that time you have a quiet time and nothing is allowed to get in the way.

Instead of the 'skip and dip' method of Scripture reading you may follow a formal reading plan. Perhaps you plan to read through the Bible in a year. (I have found the One Year Bible a great help.) Or you may have a devotional guide that picks up a thought from selected Scripture texts and then tells a related story with a moral.

Like Scripture reading, prayer in the determined phase tends to follow a predetermined pattern on a daily basis. I have one friend who has a set of prayer cards, made of small index cards, with pictures of the people he is praying for stapled to them and with concerns listed beside the picture. He goes through them each day and has found this a great help. I am not often in the determined phase; when I am, my practice is not so elaborate. I usually just have a list on a piece of paper that I keep current, scoring through names or issues as the prayers are answered, while adding new names to the bottom of the list. The advantage of having a daily set pattern is that certain people and issues receive the benefit of our consistent prayers.

Being determined about our quiet times is a necessary phase of our spiritual walk. We need to develop the discipline of meeting with the Lord regularly because of the influence of our modern world as well as our natural spiritual resistance. (Some of us are more disciplined than others. The determined quiet time is important for me because I am not one to whom discipline comes easily.) As we determine to set aside time to be with the Lord, to read Scripture and go through a set pattern of prayer, we are spiritually strengthened.

It is just like physical exercise. If we keep at our exercise, even when we don't feel like it, our body is strengthened, and we look and feel better. Likewise as we spend regular time with the Lord, even when we don't feel like it, we grow in character and are enabled to live in the conscious presence of the Lord.

While the discipline of having a regular, carefully structured quiet time has great benefits, it can also become a snare. Either we worry about skipping a day because we fear that God will be displeased with us, or we can slip into a self-satisfied attitude about doing our daily religious duty. It is easy to put a tick on the calendar and unconsciously think 'So much for God today, now on with other things.'

When we slip into either of these dangers – guilt or self-satisfaction – we will lose the pleasure of God's presence. Instead of meeting with God daily because he is delightful and wonderfully fearful, we meet with him out of habit or unhealthy fear.

It is possible to become like the older brother in the parable of the prodigal son. All the time that the younger brother was out squandering his inheritance, the older brother had been with his father. And somehow he had lost the pleasure of his father's presence. Upset when his father threw a party for the returning prodigal, his response was, 'I've been with you all this time, slaving away, doing my duty, and you've never given me a party.'

If our quiet times start to feel like a duty we are in

danger of becoming trapped in a dead habit. Instead of a loving God, he begins to seem like a task master who requires us to have a quiet time and who rejects us if we fail to live up to the standards we have set ourselves.

If you are trapped in a rigid quiet time routine that has become merely a habit, it might be good for you to skip a few days. A couple of years ago, my prayer partner mentioned that his devotional life was drying up. I made a shocking suggestion: 'Stop praying so much.' He was genuinely seeking the Lord and could handle my apparently heretical suggestion. And a month or so later he reported a freshness in his times with the Lord.

You will find that the Lord is not a legalist and he doesn't want you to become one either. His love for you is not based on whether or not you have a quiet time every day.

Study quiet time

The key distinctive of quiet times in the study phase is the serious study of Scripture. If you set aside, say, half an hour for a quiet time, at least twenty minutes of that time would be Bible study. It would not be unusual to do an in-depth study of a passage while referring to commentaries and a Bible dictionary.

When I am in this phase, rather than reading through the Scriptures in a year, I like to get a comprehensive grasp of a book or portion of Scripture. Sometimes it will be larger books like the gospels or maybe Old Testament history. I've spent over a year on each gospel, reading them through and studying them until I felt I knew each author's main point and how they had put their books together. Or I may pick a smaller book like the first letter to Peter. After a month of diligent study I generally have a grasp of the main points of the book along with some rich insights to apply to my life. Or, I may pick a portion of a book, like the Sermon on the Mount. I spent a year on the Sermon on the Mount, reading it every day until I could almost recall it word for word as I took walks.

The advantage of the study quiet time phase is that we sink our roots deep in Scripture. We provide for ourselves a rich well of spiritual truth that we can draw on throughout our lives. As we see how God works in the pages of Scripture we learn to recognize his hand in our own lives. And as we see how people responded to God in Scripture, we are inspired; to seek God as David did or to be more faithful in obedience than Saul was.

After all that time in study there is often only a little time left for prayer. Leisurely devotional worship frequently gets crowded out. Since the prayer time is cramped, it is usually short, intense and task-oriented. Prayer time easily turns into a shopping list of things we want God to do and problems we want him to solve.

It is possible, in a study quiet time, to allow our study of the Bible to become a merely mental experience. I have found that while I may be learning all kinds of information about God, I am not necessarily encountering God. We may assume that because we are studying Scripture we are actually in touch with God. The Pharisees no doubt thought the same thing. Remember, the issue for our quiet time: Am I meeting with God?

Desert quiet time

When we move into a desert quiet time phase there is a temptation to think that we have done something wrong. On the contrary. Frequently the cause is new spiritual growth encouraged by good quiet times. Surprisingly this deeper growth can lead to dryness that we didn't expect.

The desert phase is not a pleasant experience. It's like living alone in a desert. There is a feeling of empty loneliness. Our devotional life seems to dry up, and, if we feel anything at all, it is an inner sense of desolation. When we sit down to be with God, he seems absent. This longing for God and the aching sense of his absence is a common theme in the Scriptures. The psalmist writes in Psalm 42:3,

> My tears have been my food
>   day and night,
> while men say to me all day long,
>   Where is your God?

In another psalm David cries out,

> O God, you are my God,
>   earnestly I seek you;
> my soul thirsts for you,
>   my body longs for you,
> in a dry and weary land
>   where there is no water.
>   (Psalm 63:1)

And in another place he cries,

> I am worn out calling for help;
>   my throat is parched.
> My eyes fail,
>   looking for my God.
>
> (Psalm 69:3)

When this happens to us, nothing we do in our quiet time, or in any other area of life, seems right. Reading or study of Scripture is dry, there is a sawdust quality about it. The pleasure in study that we have known before is gone. Now the words on the page are nothing more than words.

Prayer too is flat. Our prayers for others seem to rise no higher than the ceiling. Worship and adoration seem a mere formality, songs that we might sing are heavy and laborious. Emotionally, there seems to be nothing inside except an aching sense of emptiness. At this point all religious affections seem gone.

Because quiet times in this phase require great effort, they tend to be practised on a periodic basis. The reason for the eight-month lapse of my quiet time referred to earlier was due to a desert period. There is both a gnawing need to meet with God and yet a frustration in the sense of his absence. This desire and frustration lead to an on-off cycle. It seems to make no difference whether we have a quiet time or not. If we have a quiet time God seems absent. If we don't have a quiet time God seems absent.

Outwardly desert quiet times and occasional quiet

times look similar. Both are erratic and inconsistent. But inwardly the two are extremely different. In the occasional phase we are erratic because God is not a priority. In the desert phase we are erratic because of an aching thirst for God that we can't seem to satisfy.

While it doesn't seem to make any difference, and although it may be very hard, maintaining a regular meeting with the Lord is important during this time. When the phase is over, we will discover wonderful benefits. I find that many things I know and teach about the Lord have come from desert times.

David benefited from and was blessed by God in the desert. He spent ten years in the desert running from Saul after God had promised David the throne. It was during this time that David learned to trust God for his promises. During this time he also developed the skills he would need to lead the nation by leading the large community of political outcasts and soldiers who came to his side in the desert.

This desert time can last for a week or two, or for years. When I was in theological college I went through a period of four years where God seemed absent. I believe that God wanted my theological learning to be more than an academic experience. In the midst of this time I began to understand why some called it 'The Dark Night of the Soul.' Don't be discouraged if it lasts a long time, there are others who have endured even longer times of dryness.

The temptation of a desert experience is to conclude that there is something wrong with us; perhaps we have sinned or are drifting away from the Lord. Or perhaps we need to read more

Scripture, or pray longer, or pray differently . . .

In fact, for those who are seeking the Lord, desert times are ones in which we are being drawn closer to him and he is doing a deep work in our hearts. We are being trained to lift our eyes from idols and earthly attachments. We learn that there is nothing, apart from the grace of God, that can satisfy our inner longings. We become detached from our earthly desires to look and long for God. In this time of physical abundance and recreational distractions how we need the ministry of the desert.

As we get closer to the Lord, we are overwhelmed with the sense of his holiness and our sinfulness. The intensity of drawing close to the Lord is like a purifying fire. While it seems that we are drying up spiritually, in fact, we are being purified and cleansed. This aching dryness of the desert continues until a work of the Spirit is completed in our hearts and we are moved into a new phase where we can take pleasure in God's presence.

While we are in a desert time, we should not be in a hurry to get out of it. God will lead us out when he is ready. Richard Foster writes, 'Be grateful that God is lovingly drawing you away from every distraction so that you can see him. Rather than chafing and fighting, become still and wait.'[1]

Devotional quiet time

In contrast to the desert phase, meeting with God in the devotional quiet time is a delight. I fear that in our attempts to seek God and to win the battle to meet with the Lord, this delight of the Lord's presence is often missed. We need to remind ourselves that spending time with God is more than a duty, or a struggle, it is a great pleasure. In the devotional quiet time we enter, in a special way, into this pleasure.

At the beginning of his Confessions, Augustine writes, 'You stimulate [us] to take pleasure in praising you, because you have made us for yourself, and our hearts are restless until they can find peace in you.' In a devotional quiet time we are invited by God to enter and enjoy this satisfying rest.

The way we read Scripture in a devotional quiet time is frequently different from the conventional approach. Rather than looking for new information or significant details in a passage, our time in Scripture has a reverent and worshipful tone.

I find it important to turn to passages that I have already studied in some depth. I spend time chewing over the verses and letting my soul soak them in until, with Paul in Ephesians, I marvel at the spiritual blessings that have been given to us through Jesus, or with Peter, I experience the unspeakable joy that I am receiving the goal of my faith, the salvation of my soul.

Sometimes it is helpful to picture yourself in the Bible passage, using your imagination to enter in to it, feeling, smelling and hearing what is happening. Many won't be comfortable with using the imagination in this way, and may prefer to miss out the next paragraph. But there is a basis to this approach because Scripture is full of images. I believe that I am honouring the Lord's intent when I take them so seriously that I give all my senses to understand and experience them.

The twenty-third psalm is a favourite of mine to handle in this way. I imagine myself in a restful green pasture, with the sun shining warmly on me, the blue sky full of drifting white clouds and a few large trees that provide just the right shade. I find myself alone with the Lord, away from the pressures that pull at me. As I settle, I find a living faith inside me that the Lord is indeed present. As I relax there, along with David I know the reality of the Lord who is restoring my soul.

While this reading of Scripture may be rich, it does not fill all of my quiet time. It is just a part of this time of meeting with God. Frequently prayer is woven into meditation on the Scriptures. Prayer in the devotional quiet time is rich and varied. There is less of a task-orientation in our prayers, there are fewer lists that we reel off for God to accomplish. While our prayers will include inter-cession there will be times of quiet listening as well. I find less than half my prayer time is taken up with petitions and intercession during such devotional times. Such prayer is important for us because, in our task-oriented age, we often ask too much of the Lord too soon. We are so busy with intercession we can miss the pleasure of just being with him.

I find that there is frequently a full silence in this devotional time, just like when I am with another person in a way that no words are necessary. I have been delighted to read Joyce Huggett's description of her experience of hearing more than a voice, of sensing a presence and soaking up the Lord's tenderness. She continues that it had never occurred to her that God wanted her to linger so he could show his delight in her.[2]

While not necessarily boisterous, the devotional quiet time is full of emotions. There is a longing hunger for the Lord and, simultaneously, a sense of being filled. You may even feel a pulling on your heart that draws you to the Lord, a calling out that doesn't cease, but only increases at his touch. Often there is a feeling of warmth, love and joy. Not infrequently there are times of anger and even fear. Running through it all there is a strong awareness of the presence of God. You know that he is with you.

The devotional quiet time generally consumes more time than other types of quiet times. There is a leisure that is required to be with the Lord in this way. Somehow five minutes turns to fifteen minutes and then even to an hour.

This sense of unhurried leisure will be uncomfortable as you first enter into a devotional quiet time. You wonder if you are merely wasting time. Perhaps you think you should be doing something more productive. If this happens, stop to remind yourself of the eternal value of being with God. If you resist the demanding voices, gradually such pressures won't seem so insistent.

When you think about the time a devotional quiet time requires, it becomes clear why we don't experience the pleasure of the Lord in this way as often as we might. Our busy lifestyles don't lend themselves to the unhurried time that a devotional quiet time requires. Like the determined and the study phases, quiet times in the devotional phase tend to be practised on a regular basis. Not perhaps every day, but several times during the week. You may take an hour or two one day and then only a brief time for the next couple of days. Breaking your routine has little effect because of the strong satisfying desire to be with God.

While all of us are called by God into such times of devotion, we may not know how to respond initially. As far back as the early years of my walk with God I remember times when I sensed a calling in my spirit to enter into times of devotion. I wasn't sure what was happening, I didn't trust my feelings and I had yet to hear teaching on the subject of a devotional life.

While the devotional quiet time is the most delightful, I have discovered that I don't stay there. Over the period of a year or two, I move back and forth from the occasional quiet time to a devotional time. Along the way I usually hit every stage in between.

A word of caution about devotional quiet times. Strange as it may sound, a devotional quiet time may not always be the best for us! In my initial enthusiasm for the delightful taste of his presence that I was discovering in fresh devotional times, I sought to open up the joys of listening to God to other people. I was surprised at the results. Some people were enriched, some were not. I discovered that unless a person had a desire to meet the Lord in this way, the pursuit of devotion stirred up emotions and expectations they weren't prepared to handle.

Further, I discovered that continuing in a devotional quiet time wasn't always appropriate. Like the disciples at the Mount of Transfiguration, it wasn't right to build a booth on the mount and dwell there. The disciples had to follow Jesus back down the mount and face the needs of the waiting crowds; and then it was on to Jerusalem and the cross.

We too have to come down from the mount. With regret, I've found that I can't expect, or demand, such divine pleasure of devotion all the time. Sometimes God gives us that delightful and deep sense of worship, sometimes he doesn't. God doesn't show up on cue, nor does he come to us in ways that we demand. He knows what we need and comes to us in ways that we can handle. The enduring reality of such pleasure in worship won't come until we see the Lord in heaven.

Temperament

Our temperaments have a great deal to do with what happens in our quiet times. I have observed that people who are methodical and detail-oriented may have a hard time getting beyond the determined quiet time, focusing rigidly on doing one's spiritual duty. On the other hand, those who tend to be more spontaneous, artistic types, for example, may skip the determined phase altogether, perhaps settling in a study quiet time for a while and then slipping back into an occasional quiet time.

I am of the spontaneous temperament. I don't like to settle into one way of doing things for very long. I have a natural inclination to avoid set daily quiet times. I handle myself in two ways. Sometimes I find it necessary to be very determined on a daily basis. At other times I make it a goal to have four or five during the week and feel good about it if I have three or four.

Whatever our quiet time experience, there is no place for self-condemnation or self-pride. When we do well, it is surely a gift of his grace to us. When we do poorly, being either irregular or legalistic, we shouldn't be surprised. God isn't. I don't condemn myself when I miss the mark. I am grateful for what times I have, I know the Lord is glad to be with me, and I determine to do better next time.

Each person has to move through the spiritual journey in his or her own way. Wherever we are in our spiritual lives, we should keep in mind that our goal in having a quiet time is to live with a heart full of devotion in the presence of God.

Conclusion

As we seek to grow in our quiet times, we must bear in mind that spiritual growth is a combination of God's initiative and our response. We can ignore, if we choose, the voice of the Spirit in our souls and his shaping of our lives. We can continue to live busy lives and banish God to the edges of our lives on the borders of consciousness. If we choose to do so we will remain in the occasional quiet time stage, thinking of God here and there and dashing off prayers in a haphazard way. If that is our response to God, our spiritual lives will remain shallow.

Or, we can be people who respond to him and find ourselves being drawn to him by some quiet inner working. As God works, we will sense a pull and call inviting us deeper. As the psalmist wrote, 'Deep calls to deep in the roar of your waterfalls' (Psalm 42:7).

As we feel this pull on our hearts, it is up to us to follow. We will find that as we grow in our responsiveness, he moves us through the dynamics of our spiritual encounters with him.

Characteristics of quiet time phases

	Occasional	Determined	Study	Desert	Devotional
Scripture	skip and dip	a regular routine	primary focus	dry	leisurely meditation
Prayer	brief, hurried, task-oriented	intercessions, thanksgiving	short, intense task-oriented	empty, forced	listening silence, intercession, worship
Emotions	up and down	satisfied	satisfied	flat, frustrated	longing hunger satisfied, fear/joy, warmth
Frequency	once in a while	regular	regular	periodic	regular
Danger	God is not the centre	legalism, complacency	academic, little time for prayer	giving up	wanting to stay there
Benefits	better than nothing	developing discipline	growth in Scripture	detached from desires	enjoying God

LISTENING TO GOD

> This is my Son, whom I love. Listen to him!
> (Mark 9:7).

> I have other sheep that are not of this sheep
> pen . . . They too will listen to my voice
> (John 10:16).

If we want a personal encounter with God, then
we must not only stop being so busy, we must
also stop talking at God so much when we pray.

It is easy to think of prayer as a monologue:
'God please do this, please take care of that.' But
a monologue is boring to the person who is forced
to listen and exhausting to the person who feels a
need to keep up the unceasing flow of words.

Today you are going to take a different approach. Resist telling God to do anything. Spend
your quiet time asking God questions and then sit
in expectation to hear what he will say.

> Speak, Lord, for I, Your servant am ready to
> hear You . . . The children of Israel said to
> Moses: Speak to us and we will hear you,
> but let the Lord not speak to us, lest
> perhaps we die for dread. Not so, Lord, not
> so, I beseech You. Rather I ask humbly with
> Samuel the prophet that you speak to me
> Yourself . . . [3]

154

Study

1. Read Habakkuk 2:1–3. What does Habakkuk say to God and how does God respond?

2. Read Psalm 32:8. Ponder God's promise of instruction. Do you expect him to instruct you?

Reflect

1. To help you listen, make a list of questions and concerns you would like God to address.

After you write them down, sit back and wait quietly to see what God will say.

2. Does it seem strange actually to listen for God to talk back? John Powell writes:

> The Lord . . . puts his ideas into my mind, and especially his perspectives. He widens my vision, helps me to see what is really important in life, and to distinguish the

really important from the unimportant . . .
He comes to me in the listening, receptive
moments of prayer, and he transfuses his
power into me.[4]

3. What did you learn from this experience?

Prayer

Ask God what he wants you to pray for and then
spend time praying for the people and concerns
that come to mind.

CHAPTER 10
QUIET TIME TOOLS

Yesterday I noticed that several door handles around our house were loose. I am not particularly handy, but I do have several screwdrivers and a small can of oil. In no time the door handles were fixed. In the same way, a few tools can keep our quiet time in good working order. We don't need to be a spiritual handyman or have a large library of biblical and theological wisdom. If the doors to our meeting with God aren't swinging open properly or there seems to be a catch in the latch, we can bring out a few spiritual tools to tighten things up and smooth out the catches.

Fasting, keeping a spiritual journal and reading Christian literature are a few of the tools that I have found especially helpful. Used wisely, these can bring depth, variety and inspiration. Fasting puts us in touch with our physical and spiritual appetites, keeping a journal sharpens our spiritual senses, and reading Christian literature puts us in touch with like-minded companions who are experienced and articulate about meeting with God.

Fasting

Fasting is a spiritual discipline that is broader than our quiet times. We may set aside half an hour for a quiet time, but a fast goes on through a day or more.

It is a helpful tool, however, because it enhances our spiritual sensitivity. Shifting our focus from the fare of the world we find that it is easier to believe that the Lord is with us, not only through the day, but especially in our quiet time. When we fast we become especially sensitive to spiritual realities and quiet times then provide an opportunity to be nourished on God's word.

What is fasting? It is abstaining from food, partially or completely, for the purpose of seeking God. The discipline of fasting, not my favourite one, occupies a significant role in the Scriptures. Sometimes fasting was used as an emergency measure when things looked desperate. David fasted when he sought God for the life of his dying child of Bathsheba (2 Samuel 12:16–23). When Judah was under attack by an overwhelming invading army, King Jehoshaphat called a national fast (2 Chronicles 20:3). And when the Jews in exile in Persia were to be killed by means of the evil political manipulation of Naaman, Mordecai and Esther called a fast to seek God for deliverance (Esther 4:16).

Sometimes fasting was used as a means of repentance, as when the exiled Jewish nation returned to the promised land under Ezra and Nehemiah (Nehemiah 9:1). The exiles discovered, as the Law was read by Ezra, how far they had departed from the ways of God. Fasting was their repentant response. Other times fasting was used as a means of dedication and preparation. Jesus spent forty days fasting in the wilderness prior to the beginning of his ministry (Matthew 4:1–4). So did Paul and Barnabas prior to their being called forth on their missionary journeys (Acts 13:1–3).

Fasting is one of the last spiritual disciplines I got round to. I like to eat and frankly wasn't interested in fasting. Because of weight problems, I have had to diet periodically and that was more than enough restraint for my liking. But while meditating on the Sermon on the Mount (Matthew 6:16–18), as Jesus taught about fasting, I realized that this too was for me.

One of the first things I noticed when I began to fast was the amazing number of advertisements that are related to food. On television, radio, magazines, hoardings, they are everywhere! 'Eat! Eat! Eat!' assaults us incessantly. The media blitz was particularly hard to resist the first time. But I find that every time I fast, my resolve to place God above my appetites is tested. Like no other discipline, fasting involves all of me, body and soul, in the pursuit of God. When my body is hungry, my appetite working overtime and my will wavering, I am reminded that I have chosen God above all my other desires. I have even found that hunger in a fast becomes my friend. Every time I feel a hunger pang it reminds me to lift my requests to God. It is the same with the ever-present adverts. Each enticement is an opportunity to say no to food and yes to God.

I fast periodically, usually during times of special needs. A couple of times I needed direction about where God was leading me in terms of my ministry and career development. One time I fasted with regard to a fund-raising deficit when I was in a para-church ministry. Then there are times when I feel out of touch with God, ministry and my family. I have found that fasting in these situations lifts my spirit and strengthens my faith. I am not particularly tied to the liturgical year, but for the past several years I have chosen to fast for Lent. I have found it a helpful aid to enter into the pain of Christ's work on the cross and then the celebration of the resurrection.

How do you actually go about fasting? On a twenty-four-hour fast I eat nothing after the evening meal until the time of the evening meal on the following day. Actually that is only missing breakfast and lunch. Unless you suffer from health problems, you should be able to handle that. A thirty-six-hour fast means eating nothing after the evening meal and skipping all meals the following day. While this is a bit more of a stretch, it is still something you should be able to do without too much difficulty. It is also possible to do a selected fast by abstaining from certain types of food. Perhaps you might skip meat for a period of time and things like coffee or chocolate. This type of fast can actually be harder than total abstinence.

It is possible and helpful to go on fasts of a longer duration. However, if you go longer than thirty-six hours it is wise to do a selective fast. Nutritionists tell me that cutting the body off from the amino acids that we get from protein for more than a day can alter the body chemistry and have a negative effect on the heart. On an extended fast I usually restrict myself to raw fruits and vegetables, along with some milk and cheese for protein. By the way, cutting out the processed fats and sugars is a healthy change to the system. In this way fasting turns out to be healthy physically as well as spiritually.

Fasting and dieting are very different. There is a power to abstain from food on a fast that isn't there when you diet. One time, towards the end of an extended fast, I was called on to work in the kitchen at a conference because of a shortage of helpers. Surprisingly, the temptation to eat was slight and I experienced a joy in serving others that wasn't natural to me. If I were dieting, I know from experience that I would not have responded with such good will or restraint.

Shortly after Jackie and I were married, an elderly neighbour invited us over. We were new in the area and we met Mrs Bibbs during one of our evening walks. We said 'Yes, of course we would love to come', and arranged a convenient time.

The agreed time was quite late, and Jackie and I thought that we were to come over for cake and coffee. However, there must have been some misunderstanding, as that was obviously not what Mrs Bibbs intended. It was clear that she had been cooking and baking all day, maybe for several days, and there it all was spread on the table for us to enjoy. But now I was not hungry. We had eaten a full meal just before we came. All that lovely food, prepared with such thoughtfulness, was not in the least appetizing to me.

We were polite, of course, and sat down to eat, profusely thanking our hostess for the wonderful meal she set before us. But the whole thing turned into a nightmare. After each serving she insisted that we have another serving and then another. Not wanting to disappoint her we ate and ate. By the time we got up from the table I was in pain and wondered if I would ever want to eat again.

Such is the way of the world. We are surrounded by people who are saying 'Have some more, have some more, have some more.' However, when we fast we are saying, 'No thank you. I'm saving room for Someone else.'

Keeping a spiritual journal

Both reading and writing have been an important part of the Christian faith. From Moses' account of the exodus, to the disciples' record of the ministry of Jesus in the gospels, to the apostle John's vision of the new heaven and earth, God's people have been directed by the Spirit to write what they experienced with God. When we write in our journal, we aren't writing inspired Scripture like they did, but we do enter into that experience of God through the written word.

In a journal, we may write down what we are thinking, feeling and learning in our meeting with God. We reflect on paper what is going on inside our hearts. We can also record our prayers and our questions for God. By doing this, we enhance our spiritual discernment of God's presence with us and his work in our lives.

Initially it may be hard to express thoughts on paper. However, I have found that writing in a journal functions as a syphon. As I write down a word or two, new words and insights come. Suddenly, the log jam breaks and the words begin to flow.

Writing in a journal helps me to pray. Sometimes I have a sense of communication with God by just going over my concerns mentally, saying my prayers in my heart. But sometimes that feels like I am only talking to myself. My remedy for that is to write out my prayers. Once I have written down what I want to say to God, then I usually have a sense that a real dialogue is taking place.

You will have to develop your own style of writing a journal. When I write out my prayers, I seldom use complete sentences. A word or a phrase on the page is usually a sufficient focal point to bring before the Lord.

When I write out my prayers, I not only record what I am asking God to do, I also put down my questions for God: 'God, what do you want me to do about . . .' Or 'God, what are you going to do about . . .?'

One day I was reading over my journal entries for several of the preceding months. It became clear that I was reading a conversation between two people. Someone was asking questions and someone else was answering! It dawned on me that my brilliant insights weren't something I could claim credit for. God was answering my questions all along and I didn't even know it.

So through keeping a journal in this way prayer can become a dialogue. In addition to asking God questions you may also write down general thoughts and ideas that come to mind during your quiet time. You may find that you will receive insights related to your questions from previous days. Write down each insight and if one raises another question, write that question out in the form of a prayer.

A great spiritual exercise is to restrict your prayers

to questions for God. Commit all your prayer concerns to him and then for a week or so, don't ask God to do anything, just ask him questions. Then be sure to allow time for recording your thoughts and insights as you study Scripture and cultivate a quiet heart. This exercise reminds us that God knows what needs to be done. We enhance our prayer life by refraining from telling him how to fix the world and solve our problems. That is why our requests can be short and to the point as Jesus teaches us to pray (Matthew 6:5–13).

Writing in a journal is a means of reflection and recognition. Writing down what we are studying and what we are feeling often produces spiritual insights. The images on a film strip are hard to see until they are reflected onto a screen. In the same way, the paper acts like a screen onto which we reflect the activities of the heart. Frequently we can see them much better and in more detail on the page.

A couple of months ago I was struggling with feelings of anger. The incident that set me off seemed insignificant: a thoughtless word from a close friend. But it set off a powder keg inside me. For a couple of days I couldn't get beyond the anger, and couldn't see why I was so angry. I tried to give it over to the Lord and let it go, but I couldn't. So I took the morning off, and went to a quiet corner at a local McDonald's and began to write. Surprisingly my anger came out as poetry. For two hours I wrote down just how mad I felt and what I wanted to do about it. I didn't censure or scold myself, I just put it all on the page. When the flurry of feeling was down on paper I eventually worked to the roots of my anger. I also found the Lord waiting for me in the depths of the pain. At that point I could let the anger go, or rather it let go of me. I then was able to make plans to respond in accordance with what I understood God required of me in Scripture.

Before I reflected on paper, the thoughts just churned around in me. My prayers concerning the anger were distracting and intruded on the rest of my quiet time. My quiet times were not quiet. When I worked out my thoughts and feelings on paper I was taking them seriously. And it was at that point that God took me seriously as well.

Recording your reflections requires some discernment. Sometimes expressing thoughts on paper is the key to interacting with God. However, sometimes it can get in the way of interacting with him. Imagine having a conversation with a good friend. In the middle of it you pull out a pen and begin to write a record of what is being said and how you are responding. That will most likely be the end of the conversation. In the same way, during our times of quiet, we may interrupt the process if we begin to write: 'Hold on, God, I'll finish worshipping you after I get a couple of thoughts down on paper.'

Sometimes a better way to use your journal is to wait till the end of your time of meditation and worship, then think back and record your reflections. In this way you honour God and can deepen your spiritual insights as you reflect back on your interaction with him. This is a way of recognizing God. We recognize, or think again, about our times with him. And when we do, we see with new insights into the ways that God is working within us.

Practical details

Keeping a journal can be as formal as writing in a bound notebook that you keep to review in later years, or as informal as writing on sheets of paper that you throw away once you are finished the day's quiet time. I have used both and found both helpful. Keeping journal notebooks that you review in later years can be encouraging because they provide a written record of your pilgrimage with God. By looking over them you can see where you have grown and what you have learned, as well as what you have forgotten and need to learn again.

Writing on sheets of paper that are thrown away once your quiet time is over can be very freeing. You know that you are not writing for the sake of posterity, yours or anyone else's! You just put down in phrases or words what you are feeling or asking God to do. When you write on journal sheets in this way you are reminding yourself that it is the interaction with God that is the important thing. Once you have expressed yourself to God on paper, then your purpose is served.

If you do keep your journal sheets, in a folder or a note book, be sure to date each entry, the day, week and year. Sometimes I also put the place. We have done a fair amount of moving and it is interesting to look back on past thoughts and recall what I was learning while living in Atlanta, Jackson, Nashville or London.

As with all spiritual disciplines and tools, don't be legalistic about keeping a journal. You may want to keep it daily. That's great. But perhaps you only write in a journal a couple of times a week or a couple of times a month. That's great too. Both offer opportunities to reflect and record the work of God in your heart.

Christian literature

The writers of divinely inspired Scripture are not the only ones to have written about their thoughts and experiences with God. Christians throughout the ages have recorded their own insights and experiences. When we read what they wrote we discover inspiring companions that can enrich our quiet times.

Some books were written to be used as devotionals – as aids to worship. The most famous is probably *The Imitation of Christ* by Thomas à Kempis. Written just before the Reformation, it has been used by Catholics and, in a rewritten and adjusted form, by Protestants ever since. Each day there is a bite-sized thought that is filled with practical spiritual wisdom. The Catholic edition has a couple of passing references to purgatory and a section of meditations on the Lord's Supper – the Mass. Most Protestant versions leave out this section and delete the passages on purgatory. The fact that Puritans, Pietists and Protestants of every generation have found it worth 'sanitizing' is a testimony to its continuing value.

One of the most widespread devotional guides of the twentieth century is *My Utmost for His Highest* by Oswald Chambers. I know people who work through it and then turn around and start it all over again. Then there are a vast number of devotional magazines. I especially like the material produced by *Scripture Union*. It seeks to be contemporary, biblical and practical.

The danger of using a devotional guide is that we can treat it like spiritual fast-food. We read the bite-sized thought, glance at the Scripture reference and then we are off to take on the day. What happened to meeting with God?

The benefit of using a guide is that we are invited into fellowship with another Christian who has some insight and experience of God. If we take the time, we can meet God in fellowship with the author in ways that enhance our own personal spiritual encounter.

Some books were written to teach us how to cultivate a devotional life. The earliest devotional manual ever written was *The Conferences of Cassian*. In the fifth century Cassian travelled around the Egyptian desert and Palestine interviewing monks. He put together a record of those conversations and in so doing formed the basis for all spiritual instruction manuals to follow.

Since Cassian, thousands of instructional manuals have been written. Twentieth-century authors whose instructional books have been helpful to me in tapping into the wisdom of early spiritual guides are A. W. Tozer, Richard Foster, Henri Nouwen, Joyce Huggett and Eugene Peterson. For specific titles see suggestions for further study in the appendix.

Reading these and other instructional works can enhance a quiet time, not just because they give information on how to have a quiet time, but because they contain a spirit of devotion. In reading about how to pray there is an inspiration to pray. We are drawn to God in a way that makes us want to pray.

Finally I want to mention books that weren't written to be used as devotionals, or instructions on the devotional life, but which nevertheless, can be inspirations and aids to worship. I am reading a book right now by a contemporary theologian. In the morning, with a cup of coffee and my journal, I leisurely read a couple of pages on my back porch. As I read, I am inspired to think about God, to appreciate God and to grow in my thought-life about God. Every few sentences I stop to savour a thought and the freshness of the morning. My own thoughts of God are stretched as I appreciate a brother in Christ who is loving God with his mind and heart.

The great works of the teachers through the ages can be read this way: *The Confessions of Augustine*, Calvin's *The Institutes of Christian Religion*, *The Works of Luther*, *The Journals of Wesley*, and Jonathan Edwards' *Religious Affections* to mention a few. These people, and others like them, had great thoughts about and great experiences of God. Reading them we are taken deeper in to the knowledge of God than we could ever go on our own. Standing on their shoulders we get a better glimpse of heaven then we would by standing on our own two feet.

THE REVELATION OF JESUS CHRIST

Revelation 1:1–3

Frankly, I'm surprised at the positive attitude towards the Bible that is still present in our culture. Although subjected to all kinds of criticism over the past century, a large number still believe that the Bible is more than merely a human book, and that it has merit for the historical and cultural insights it gives on religion. Even those who are not regular churchgoers or diligent Bible students believe that there is something special about it.

A friend of ours tells stories about his colourful grandfather and the Bible. On occasion he would cause a crowd to gather by pointing to a piece of cloth he had dropped on the pavement and shouting, 'It's alive!' When people stopped to see what he was pointing at, he would lift up the cloth to reveal a Bible. Taking up the Bible and waving it in the air above his head he would preach to his listeners about the virtues of the Bible.

The Bible is alive. Something happens when you read it. The words on the page are more than nice ideas or guidelines for moral behaviour. It's more than a theology textbook. Something reaches up from the page to address the mind and the heart. Something or Someone comes through the words to call and challenge, to provoke, stimulate and entice. It is similar to what the two disciples on the road to Emmaus experienced after they met the Lord on the resurrection day, 'Were not our hearts burning within us while he talked with us on the road and opened the Scriptures to us?' (Luke 24:32).

As you read the book of Revelation, it is possible that you may enter into the same experience as the disciples on the road to Emmaus. The one who spoke the book to John, may, if you ask him, lift the words from the page and speak them to you. When that happens they will feed your soul, shape your thoughts and strengthen your heart.

Approach

In Revelation 1:3, there is a blessing offered to those who read, hear and take to heart the book of Revelation. Plan to read it silently and out loud and think about it during your quiet time and later during the day. Read it out loud now and write a prayer asking the Lord to allow you to take it to heart.

Study

1. Read Revelation 1:1–3. What different means of communication are used in the verses?

2. Who are the people involved in sending and receiving the revelation?

3. What assurance are we given that the messages about the future are trustworthy?

4. The revelation is about 'what must soon take place'. There are a number of different ways to interpret this. Godly and scholarly commentators have different opinions. What do you think? Do you think 'soon' means:

   a. In the next couple of years of the first century?

   b. What will happen throughout the unfolding history of the church?

   c. What will happen at the end of time?

   d. All the preceding?

Reflection

1. The word revelation means 'uncovering'. The book of Revelation is not merely about the

future in general, it is about the revealing of Jesus Christ. Imagine that there is a veil across your heart. Ask the Lord to remove it so that you may see his presence in your life. Sit for a while and allow him to work. Write down your impressions and emotions.

2. The time-frame of the revelation is the impending future. Jesus wants us to know what is going to happen so we can live and think accordingly. How would your behaviour be affected if you knew what Jesus was going to do in your life within the next week or so? Consider your work, your family, your friends, your time and your money.

Pray

Ask the Lord to come back soon.

Ask the Lord to give you a sense of anticipation for his return.

Pray that several fellow believers will grow in a love for God's word.

CHAPTER 11
QUIET TIME DISCIPLESHIP

Dave greeted me in the hall one Wednesday night. In a very casual manner he asked if I had a few minutes to talk. After a full evening of teaching I was not especially eager to do so. I thought about asking him to phone me in the morning. But there are those moments when it's wise to change the schedule. I sensed this was one of them. His casual manner was covering up anxiety.

It had recently dawned on Dave that his relationship with God had always been through others. As a boy it was the church youth group. As an adult, it was through his wife and the associations he gained through leadership in the church. He was only now realizing that he hoped that would be enough. And in the past it had been.

Now all that was changing. God was calling Dave to come face to face with him. I knew I didn't need to instruct or admonish him, just open up a spiritual door. So we spent some quiet time together. Through the veil of other people and busy activities the Lord stepped in to meet him. In the quiet, Dave gave over to God his wife, daughter, work, church activities and his business. And there in the quiet, Dave's second-hand experience became a personal embrace of love between God and his son. If I had merely given Dave a pep-talk on Christian commitment and sent him on his way, I don't think that the meeting or the divine surrender would have taken place. But in the quiet, he was able to make a life-changing personal commitment.

Through the use of quiet time with God, people like Dave learn that Jesus Christ himself is there to meet us, lead us and disciple us.

A couple of years into ministry work, it dawned on me that my focus was out. Working with college students, I taught Bible-study skills, evangelism, leadership development, small-group dynamics, apologetics and ways to think Christianly. Several of my campus groups were active in social justice issues in the inner city. Some of the students were seeking to develop a simple lifestyle. This was all exciting and done in the name of the Lord. But something was wrong. God was not the focus of my ministry. Jesus was an assumed presence. I wasn't ministering a knowledge drawn from God, I was imparting skills and teaching contemporary Christian issues.

In looking for another approach, I wondered if quiet times might shift the focus. I invited Ned to meet me at 7:30 a.m. in the student union. We chose a small room, closed the door and spent half an hour in quiet. We both had our Bibles and note pads. Before we began we agreed we wouldn't talk until our half-hour was over. We read Scripture, prayed and then cultivated an attitude of listening silence.

As we began, I was uncomfortable. I felt responsible to make this quiet time work. I was the 'discipler' and Ned was the disciple. Shortly into the quiet time, I was able to let go of my false sense of responsibility. I realized that Jesus was the discipler, not me. At that point, my restless silence was replaced by a restful peace. It was as if I invited Ned to meet a friend. After introducing them I was to get out of the way and let them talk.

After that experience with Ned I began to invite several students each term to have quiet times with me. Most of the time these were spiritually powerful experiences. However, there were occasions when quiet-time discipling produced a negative reaction. Some people didn't like it, some were even offended and thereafter kept their distance. I learned that I needed to be selective, looking for those who were hungry for a personal encounter with the Lord and were willing to be stretched in that way.

When we use quiet times as a discipling tool, we function as a spiritual guide while those to whom we minister grow in discernment. For a term, the student leadership team at a university in the South met weekly to share a group quiet time. They called themselves a 'listening team'. Each quiet time session was opened with the question, 'Lord, how do you want us to serve you?' After twenty minutes of quiet time there was an open discussion. None of us received a flaming vision. But over the course of the term, the group sensed that they were being led to evangelism. Not everyone was eager to do this. But from our quiet time together there was a shared awareness of calling. Doing evangelism wasn't just a good idea, it was what the Lord himself was calling us to do.

As the leader in the group, I was not the source of vision. Through the quiet time, they 'heard' from the Lord, not me. On the other hand, in the quiet times,

I was more than an appendage. My role was to call us to the Lord as we began, and then, during our discussions after our quiet time, to see that we measured our perceptions against the background of Scripture and sound doctrine. Christian leadership is not so much doing, or getting others to do, things for God. Rather it is taking the lead in seeking to discern what he is doing so that together we can respond to it and participate in it.

While not as elaborate or extended as that student meeting, in our church's monthly leadership meetings there are times when we use a brief quiet time. When our direction is not clear, or when there is sharp disagreement, we may choose to spend time in silence. During this quiet time, we give over our concerns to the Lord and seek to listen for his direction. Afterwards, we debrief. This discernment process has not produced unanimous decisions, but it has got us over impasses and through a few tense conflicts. The focus is put back on the Lord as the head of the church, from whom we seek direction. As we seek God in the quiet we are rescued from acting as merely a corporate board in which issues are pondered and decisions made.

Using quiet time as a discipling tool rescues us from an unhealthy dependence on technique and method. We are becoming a technique-oriented culture and it is natural to adopt a technique approach to ministry. However, when quiet time is used as a discipling tool, it takes the focus off technique. We are meeting with the Lord and he is the one we expect to direct us and bless our efforts.

When we base our ministry in quiet time, the issue becomes not how to do it, but *who* is doing it.

Using quiet time as a discipling tool rescues spiritually hungry hearts from false activism. Occasionally someone comes to me with a desire to do more for the Lord. This is exciting, but potentially dangerous. Their expectation is that I will give them a job to do, help them start a ministry or put them on a committee. If I can help it, I don't do any of those. Instead, I suggest that the most important thing that they can do for the Lord is get to know him better and I tell them about quiet time.

Once they are established in meeting with God, then they are in a position to minister. If I give them a job, a committee assignment or allow them to begin a ministry before they have a pattern of meeting with God, they may continue in the mistaken belief that doing things for God is an acceptable substitute for cultivating a personal relationship with him. In the end, that is the road to spiritual frustration and burnout.

Quiet time can also be a powerful tool for evangelism. When people are open to believing in God, but aren't sure that he is really there, quiet times can open spiritual doors. In response to the inevitable question, 'How do I know that there really is a God?' my response is, 'Ask him, he'll tell you himself.' I instruct potential converts to set aside some time to explore knowing God. They begin by simply speaking into the air and asking God to make himself known. Then I tell them to read a portion of one of the gospels. In addition they are to keep a journal of their thoughts about God for a week or two. Finally they are to keep their eyes open for 'God-incidents', those coincidental circumstances that let us know that someone is working in the events of our lives.

For those spiritually hungry enough to take up my challenge, the conversion rate, while not one hundred per cent, is high. In a follow-up meeting I find that they either have already given their lives to the Lord or are looking forward to praying a prayer of commitment with me.

In doing evangelism in this way I find I function as a witness on two different levels. First, I testify about my own experiences with the Lord and tell them that the same opportunity is open to them. Second, when they come to me and tell me about their spiritual encounters I get to witness the work of God's Spirit in them. As I listen to them, my role is to affirm what Jesus himself is doing and clarify questions that they may have.

Those who come into the Christian faith in this way know for certain that they have a personal relationship with the living God, and are not merely ascribing to a set of beliefs. They know that Jesus is here and can communicate with them. Having begun their spiritual life through a meeting with God, the continuation of a regular quiet time seems the most natural thing in the world.

Means

Encouraging people to spend time with God is one of the most strategic things we can do for our church. What would the church be like if the majority of its members had quiet times each week? How can we go about a quiet time ministry?

It is important to encourage quiet times by sharing one. Not knowing any better, beginners may read the Bible and pray, but have no expectation of personal encounter with God. Nor will they be able to settle enough inwardly to cultivate the sense of quiet so necessary for a meeting with God. However, when they are invited to meet with the Lord with someone who knows what this is, they get a taste for it. Once they know what it is like, they can go on to satisfy a tantalized appetite on their own.

In using quiet times as a discipling tool, early mornings are best. The only time many people can meet is before they go to work. For a year Will, Carl, Todd and I met together each Friday morning from 6 a.m. to 7 a.m. in a lounge at church. We worked through a couple of quiet-time guides together. As long as we were finished by seven o'clock they were able to get to work in time. Their experience of quiet times on Friday spilled over to the rest of the week. Todd started having quiet times with his wife before heading off to work. Carl started getting to work early and shutting the door for half an hour for his quiet time. All three were already involved in ministries at the church, but I believe there was a noticeable change in the tone of their ministries as they spoke more of the relational dimension of Christianity, the possibility of a personal knowledge of God.

Meeting Todd, Carl and Will together worked well for a couple of reasons. For one thing, having quiet times more than once or twice a day with others leaves me spiritually and physically drained. It is delightful, satisfying and exhausting. By meeting as a small group of four, I was able to extend the reach of a quiet time ministry. Another benefit was that the group quiet time and the sharing afterwards enriched the diversity of our experience of God's presence and allowed the opportunity of mutual affirmation.

When we disciple by means of a quiet time we are engaged in an exciting, revolutionary action. When Moses approached Pharaoh to let Israel go from their bondage and slavery, he asked that Israel be allowed to go into the desert for three days to worship God. Pharaoh was not pleased and the battle began. By means of a quiet time we follow Moses, inviting people to come out from the world to meet God in the desert.

In quiet times as a means of discipleship, to shift the image, we invite God out of cultural exile and back into a daily immersion in our lives. By the practice of a quiet time we know him as present: Immanuel – God with us.

THE FINAL MEAL WITH <u>CHRIST</u>

John 13:1–17

Getting ready to go

Today as you read these verses from John 13 you are entering into a sacred experience. You will be standing on holy ground. Jesus is going to die. He is within hours of the cross and he is spending these last moments with those who have been most dear to him on earth. Every word that comes out of his mouth during this final conversation will be remembered, thought about and meditated upon by those who hear them. Every action will be relived in the minds of those who have loved and followed him.

Often, people who know that they are dying withdraw into themselves. Their pain, loss, grief, and fear are all-consuming. But Jesus continued to love. Above all, he wanted his followers to know that they were loved and he demonstrated this love freely in word and action.

As a lover of Jesus, enter into this holy moment. Look. Listen. Feel. Prepare yourself to experience in a new way 'the full extent of his love'.

Approach

Jesus wants you to know his love. What words or ideas come to mind when you think of the love of God?

How would you evaluate your sense of the Lord's love?
Do you think you may have:

● a better emotional experience than intellectual understanding of the Lord's love for you – a stronger heart?

● a better intellectual understanding than emotional experience – a more mature mind?

● a good balance between the intellectual and the emotional – a strong heart and a mature mind?

Study

1. After reading John 13:1–5 for background, focus on verse 1. What does Jesus know and what light does it cast on the impending events?

2. The events to come take place against the background of the Passover. Look up the following verses in Exodus and summarize them in your own words.

    Exodus 12:12–13

Exodus 12:21–23

Exodus 12:29–30

3. How do these verses from Exodus help you understand what Jesus was facing?

4. As he writes about forthcoming events, John does not mention that Jesus is about to be crucified and die. Why not?

Reflect

1. What might Jesus have been feeling as he faces his disciples and the future?

2. At some time or other we have all had to say goodbye to people we love. Recall some of your most difficult goodbyes to those you loved and didn't want to leave. Write down who you were separated from and some of the thoughts and feelings you experienced.

3. Imagine that you are about to finish your time in the world and are soon to be with your heavenly father. What concerns would you have?

Prayer

Pray that God would give you a spirit of wisdom and revelation so that you might know him better.

Ask God to bless your friendship with fellow Christians, that you might begin growing in a mutual love for each other.

CHAPTER 12

BECOMING A QUIET PERSON

There are several hats I wear. Depending on the time of day and who I am with, I am a father, a husband, a pastor, a friend, a brother or a son. On some days, I change hats easily and without much thought. But there are times when I become aware of the burdens of responsibility.

Today I don't feel like I've done such a good job of balancing my role as a pastor and a father. As my two older boys are moving into the last stages of school there are times when I feel at a loss to give them what a father should. Part of the reason I struggle with this is that I am away from them more than I should be, it seems.

On the other hand, there is more to do at the church than can possibly be done. I'm grateful that I am a member of a vital church and there are two other pastors and a number of lay leaders with whom I share ministry responsibilities. Still, there are tasks to which I should be giving myself that are not being done.

On days like today, when I am feeling the pull of competing responsibilities, I have a choice. I can let them press me down into some pretty painful feelings, or let them take me down to my knees in prayer. Today, I chose to pray. Calling out this morning in my quiet time, I was met with a sense of presence. Praying through the activities and agendas of the past week, I began to see the ways in which God has been active and with me. I felt my spirit lift as I realized that God was meeting, shaping and challenging me to new growth. After my quiet time, I didn't feel any more competent than I did before I started, but I knew that the responsibilities weren't mine alone. There was a quiet sense of peace in the place where before there had been a feeling of anxiety.

Spending time with God makes a difference in our lives, right down to the depths of our character. You could say that investing in a quiet time makes one into a quiet person. In contrast to many Christians, who are driven by the world in which we are immersed, a quiet person has a strength of character that allows him or her to live a more considered and paced way of life.

You might misunderstand what I mean by a quiet person. I'm not talking about someone who only speaks occasionally, or someone who is passive and withdrawn, or a shrinking-violet sort of person who sits in a corner. On the contrary, a quiet person is active and productive. Nor do I mean someone who never gets excited, upset or angry. It is the very opposite. A quiet person still feels anger, indignation, frustration, fear, desire and more. What makes a quiet person different is that these emotions are experienced in the context of time alone with God. In the quiet of God the emotions age and work on our hearts to produce a Spirit-directed maturity.

The biblical picture of a quiet person

Abraham, Moses, David and Jesus are among those who were quiet people. They didn't all start out being quiet. It is what they became as they grew in the knowledge of God.

Abraham became a quiet person. Through the years of his walk with God he moved from actions of cowardice, in twice denying that Sarah was his wife, to the courage necessary to offer Isaac as a sacrifice at God's command. Despite the anxiety he must have felt over the impending death of his son, he trusted God enough to believe that he would raise him from the dead. On his walk to the mount of sacrifice there was no cold resistance to God, rather a quiet, determined obedience. When Isaac asked where the sacrifice is, he could reply with confidence, 'God himself will supply it'.

Moses moved from a rage that led to the murder of an Egyptian slave driver – an attempt that would have made him a false deliverer – to a disciplined heart of the real deliverer of Israel. There were a number of times in his life when his anger broke out: when he smashed the tablets of the Law over the golden calves, or when he lashed out at the rock when the people failed to trust God for his provision. But he grew. In words that were written towards the end of his life we can pick up a quiet tone: 'Teach us to number our days aright, that we may gain a heart of wisdom' (Psalm 90:12).

David too was a quiet person. In the midst of a life of fighting giants, leading armies, uniting his country and establishing a dynasty, he found time to write psalms of reflective worship. With him more than anyone else we get a glimpse into a quiet heart. On the one hand he can write, 'The Lord is my shepherd, I shall not want . . .' Then he can turn around and write, 'My life is consumed by anguish and my years by groaning; my strength fails because of my affliction and my bones grow weak' (Psalm 31:10).

Jesus is a quiet person. Confronting the hostile religious leaders, demanding the submission of shouting demons, sleeping in the midst of a storm while the disciples panicked, imploring God in Gethsemane or calling out from the cross, in all these situations he lived from a quiet heart. Jesus describes himself as one who is 'gentle and humble in heart' (Matthew 11:29). Isaiah foretells Jesus' character. Speaking of the coming messiah he writes, 'He will not shout or cry out or raise his voice in the streets. A bruised reed he will not break, and a smoldering wick he will not snuff out' (Isaiah 42:2–3). It is from this place of quiet that Jesus invites us to 'find rest for your souls' (Matthew 11:29).

The benefits of being a quiet person

Living from the quiet there is no need for a mask, facade or appearances. These quiet people of Scripture had a settledness, an authenticity, an integration of the inward and the outward. They were not hypocrites, showing one face to the world while hiding another face with a different disposition.

Being a quiet person is a predisposition of character. There is no need to be in control or controlling. Nor is there a need to be manipulative, competitive or demanding. A quiet person can be firm, express disappointments, ask for what he or she wants and advocate what is important. This freedom comes from the experience of quiet time with God. As we spend time with him, our souls and the cells of our bodies know that Jesus is the Lord, and that he is working in the circumstances, whatever they are, for his glory and our good.

When we learn to be quiet people we find that, while we are more integrated between the inner and the outer aspects of our person, we still live on two levels. On one level we can be coping with the day-to-day experiences of life, driving a car, talking to a friend, working at our desk. At another level we can have an underlying sense of the presence of God. Somewhere deep inside we know that God is with us, indeed within us. We sense that he is supporting us even while we know that we are submitted to his authority and are living in obedient response to him as we have responded to Jesus' invitation to take his yoke upon us (Matthew 11:29).

Learning to be quiet doesn't mean that our lives will be easy. Just as every quiet person in Scripture lived in the midst of turbulence and struggle, so you will too. Perhaps you will have to face the sickness and death of loved ones unexpectedly. Maybe you will face career obstacles that will stand in the way of deeply held hopes and dreams. It is possible your hopes for a happy home and a 'perfect' marriage will be marred by past pains and patterns that produce current frustration rather than affection. What will make the difference in your life will be the way you choose to face these battles. The issue is spending enough time with God so that the quiet works its way inside.

As we spend time quietly with God there comes an alteration. We find a willing submission to God and satisfaction in his presence. Along with a rest and refreshment there comes a sense of guidance, direction, protection and provision by our Shepherd.

Once we have experienced that inner quiet, then even in the midst of 'the valley of the shadow of death' there can be a settled courage. This experience of quiet is more than cognitive. It is a way of being. The quiet moves from outside us to inside us, invading us as we are immersed in it. I believe that this is what Paul had in mind when he wrote, 'Do not be anxious about anything, but in everything, by prayer and petition, with thanksgiving, present your requests to God. And the peace of God, which transcends all understanding, will guard your hearts and your minds in Christ Jesus' (Philippians 4:6–7).

Keeping at it

If you don't experience the effects of being quiet right away, don't be discouraged or give up. Years of poor habits of spiritual nurture and hectic schedules take their toll on our souls. If you are spending some time in quiet each day, and it still seems that the Lord is absent, it may be that you will have to extend your time with God. Perhaps for a while you need to move from twenty minutes to forty-five, or more, with occasional times of even longer duration.

I sponsor three-hour retreats of silence at our church on occasional Sunday afternoons. When I first began to offer these only a few brave souls came. Everyone wondered what in the world they would do with three hours of silence! However, after the experience, almost all commented that even three hours wasn't long enough! Afterwards many find that there is a different quality to their time with God, a more tangible sense of his 'being there'.

If we are to become spiritually healthy people, then we have to change our spiritual chemistry. Over the past four years I put on 10 inches around my waist and at least 40 pounds. Through poor and half-hearted diets and irregular exercise I messed up my metabolism and increased the fat-to-muscle ratio in my body. When I first sought to get in shape through a better diet, the results weren't great. Initially I didn't lose any weight. Then I began walking two miles a day. Only a few of pounds came off and then I stabilized at 35 pounds above my desired weight. This was not good.

So then I began walking four miles a day. Still nothing, except that I could begin to eat normally without putting on weight. Then I began to run three miles a day. After two months of this, still nothing! More needed to be done. Middle age was taking its toll. Only when I began a routine of regular running over three miles did my body chemistry alter in such a way that my weight began to drop. It was necessary to increase my metabolic rate for over forty-five minutes a day plus cutting down on my fat intake before my system would began to alter the way it processed my food. As my system changed, with my cardiovascular system improving, the outward effects began to show in reduced inches around my waist.

I believe that there is a direct parallel in my weight loss experience and our quiet times. If we are spiritually out of shape we shouldn't look for immediate results. We must just keep at it. If we spend time with God, eventually the spiritual conditioning of our hearts will show itself in ways that we and others will be able to see.

Relax and be quiet

Whatever you do in your efforts to become a quiet person, be gentle and gracious with yourself. Don't push too hard or be too demanding. I remember teaching my sons how to swim. Before the lessons could begin in earnest, they had to get used to the water. As we got into the shallow end of the pool, there was a lot of clinging and kicking. Once they relaxed, they found that they could put their feet down and stand. Once that happened, everything changed. They began to enjoy the water. Only then could I begin the lessons.

You too need to relax. Your heavenly Father has brought you into the water of life. Instead of clinging to him in a state of panic, let go and trust him. You will find that he will lead you in your spiritual lessons. As he spoke through the psalmist thousands of years ago, he still speaks '*Be still and know that I am God*' (Psalm 46:10).

LEARNING TO BE A QUIET <u>PERSON</u>

Psalm 23

Drawing on the book *Moby Dick* by Herman Melville, Eugene Peterson calls our attention to the power and effectiveness of a quiet person.

> . . . there is a turbulent scene in which a whaleboat scuds across a frothing ocean in pursuit of a great, white whale, Moby Dick. The sailors are laboring fiercely, every muscle taut, all attention and energy concentrated on the task . . . In this boat, however, there is one man who does nothing. He doesn't hold an oar; he doesn't perspire; he doesn't shout. He is languid in the crash and cursing. This man is the harpooner, quiet, poised and waiting. And then this sentence: 'To insure the greatest efficiency in the dart, the harpooners of this world must start to their feet out of idleness, and not out of toil.'[1]

Being quiet does not mean we aren't doing anything. Nor does being quiet mean that we aren't being effective and productive. The harpooner had to be rested and quiet so that he would be ready to act at the right time. Through Isaiah God says, 'In repentance and rest is your

salvation. In quietness and trust is your strength'
(Isaiah 30:15).

Psalm 23 uses the images of the land rather than
the sea to convey the important effects of being
quiet. The point is the same. If we spend time in
the 'green pastures' and 'in the house of the Lord',
then we will find that we can rise to the challenges
of life; whether it be a white whale in the sea or a
nameless, faceless enemy in some dark valley of
the shadow of death.

Approach

Write out the twenty third psalm, copy it word for
word. As you write it out, personalize it so you
know that it applies to you. You might like to
replace 'my' and 'me' with your name.

Study

1. David declares that God is his Shepherd. In what specific ways does David experience this?

2. In what ways does David respond to God's caring presence?

3. What do you think is the meaning of the phrase, 'I shall lack nothing' (verse 1).

4. David portrays God's presence in three contrasting situations, 'green pastures' (verse 2), the 'valley of the shadow of death' (verse 4), and a battlefield (verse 5). How does God meet David's need in each?

5. David writes that he will 'dwell in the house of the LORD for ever' (verse 6). Since the temple had not yet been built, what do you think he means?

Reflection

1. I summarized each verse in my own words like this:

   Verse 1 – submission and satisfaction
   Verse 2 – rest and refreshment
   Verse 3 – guidance and direction
   Verse 4 – confidence and comfort
   Verse 5 – protection and provision
   Verse 6 – presence and peace

   Now you give it a try using your own words. Or, if you like mine, personalize the phrases like this: for verse 1 you might write, 'I choose to submit to the Lord as my Shepherd and be satisfied in the ways that he leads me.'

2. Imagine that you are in a place of green grass, blue sky and quiet water. Sit there until you find the quiet working its way inside you. Write down how it affects you and how it affects your sense of God's presence.

3. God is a shepherd who guides us. It is when we are quiet that we can discern his leading, and respond to it. Think back through the past week or so. How do you think the Lord may have been guiding you?

4. David says that God makes him lie down in green pastures. Has God ever put you in a situation where you have had to slow down?

How did you respond?

Prayer

Pray that your church will find ways to create green pastures, places where people can spend time being quiet with the Lord.

Ask God to make you a quiet person that lives in a responsive way to his shepherding.

'The strength
of a good soldier
of
Jesus Christ
appears in
nothing more
than in
steadfastly maintaining
the
holy calm,
meekness,
sweetness
and
benevolence
of
his mind,
amidst
all the
storms,
injuries,
strange behavior
and
surprising acts
and
events
of this
evil
and
unreasonable
world.'[2]

NOTES

Chapter 1: Becoming a quiet person

1. J. I. Packer, *Knowing God* (Hodder & Stoughton, 1973), p. 14.
2. Jonathan Edwards, *Religious Affections* (Banner of Truth, 1986), p. 305.
3. A. W. Tozer, *The Pursuit of God* (Send the Light, 1987), p. 18.

Chapter 2: Why we need quiet times

1. Stephen Eyre, *Defeating the Dragons of the World* (IVP/USA, 1987), p. 127.

Chapter 3: What is a quiet time?

1. A. W. Tozer, *The Pursuit of God*, p. 18.
2. Jonathan Edwards, *Religious Affections*, p. 305.
3. Gerald May, *Addiction and Grace* (Harper-SanFrancisco, 1988), p. 1.

Chapter 4: Settling in God's presence

1. Richard Foster, *Meditative Prayer* (Marc Europe, 1985), p. 15.

Chapter 6: Getting alone with God

1. Martin Luther, quoted in Donald Bloesch, *The Struggle of Prayer* (Harper & Row, 1980), p. 63.

Chapter 7: Following a quiet time pattern

1. John White, *People in Prayer* (IVP, 1978), p. 12.
2. Martin Luther, quoted in Donald Bloesch, *The Struggle of Prayer*, (Harper & Row, 1980), p. 63.
3. Joyce Huggett, *Listening to God* (Hodder & Stoughton, 1986), pp. 33–34.
4. Jonathan Edwards, *Religious Affections*, p. 192.
5. J. I. Packer, *Knowing God*, p. 56.
6. Basil Pennington, quoted in Joyce Huggett, *Listening to God*, p. 158.
7. A. W. Tozer, *The Pursuit of God* (Send the Light, 1987), p. 76

Chapter 9: Quiet time dynamics

1. Richard Foster, *Celebration of Discipline* (Hodder & Stoughton, 1989), p. 91.
2. Joyce Hugget, *Listening to God*, pp. 33–34
3. Thomas à Kempis, *The Imitation of Christ* (Hodder & Stoughton, 1979).
4. John Powell, quoted in Joyce Huggett, *Listening to God*, p. 27.

Chapter 12: Becoming a quiet person

1. Eugene Peterson, *The Contemplative Pastor* (Word, 1989), p. 33.
2. Jonathan Edwards, *Religious Affections*, p. 278.

FOR FURTHER READING

Abiding in Christ's love by Stephen and Jacalyn Eyre (Scripture Union, 1996). A month of guided quiet times in John 13 – 17, looking at what it means to have a personal relationship with a heavenly Lord.

Sinking your roots in Christ by Stephen and Jacalyn Eyre (Scripture Union, 1996). Selected portions of the book of Revelation with meditations on how to live now in the light of our heavenly future.

Sitting at the feet of Jesus by Stephen and Jacalyn Eyre (Scripture Union, 1996). A month of guided quiet times in the Sermon on the Mount, looking specifically at what it means to be a disciple living under the lordship of Christ.

Waiting on the Lord by Stephen and Jacalyn Eyre (Scripture Union, 1996). A month of guided quiet times in Psalms 30 – 40, with encouragement to trust God.

Spiritual Encounters by Stephen Eyre (Frameworks, 1991). A month of guided quiet times on selected portions of Scripture, giving the basic skills and experience of spiritual disciplines used in a quiet time.

Listening to God by Joyce Huggett (Hodder, 1986).
A helpful personal reflection on the process of
turning prayer into a two-way conversation rather
than a one-way monologue.

Too busy not to pray by Bill Hybels (IVP, 1988).
Valuable guidelines for a rich, consistent prayer life,
recognizing the struggles of finding time.

Rooted in God's Love by Dale and Juanita Ryan (IVP,
1992). Meditations for the broken-hearted, the
crushed in spirit, those who have been battered by
life's storms.

Prayer: Finding the heart's true home by Richard
Foster (Hodder, 1992).

Celebration of Discipline by Richard Foster (Hodder,
1989).

Praying with Jesus by Eugene Peterson (Harper
SanFrancisco, 1994).

The Contemplative Pastor by Eugene Peterson
(Eerdmans, 1993).

My Utmost for His Highest by Oswald Chambers
(Nova Publishing, 1989).

The Imitation of Christ by Thomas à Kempis
(Hodder, 1979).